This Far By Faith

Twenty Years At Cass Community

Faith Fowler

Cass Community Publishing House
an imprint of
David Crumm Media, LLC
Canton, Michigan

For more information and further discussion, visit
www.ccpublishinghouse.org
Study guides for *This Far By Faith* will be avaliable online in
late 2014.

Cover photo by Joe Craciola
CCPH logo by Winnifred Covintree
Map of Detroit by Dick DeRonne

Cover art and design by
Rick Nease
www.RickNeaseArt.com

Published by
Cass Community Publishing House
an imprint of
David Crumm Media, LLC
42015 Ford Rd., Suite 234
Canton, Michigan, USA

For information about customized editions, bulk purchases or
persmissions, contact Cass Community Publishing House at
TFBF@casscommunity.org.

Contents

Dedicated to Dr. Viola Reeves and Sally Fowler.

Introduction

After 20 years at Hull House, Jane Addams wrote a memoir describing her life and work. In so many ways, I am no Jane Addams. She was obviously stationed in Chicago and I'm in Detroit. She dealt with the abhorrent conditions in factories and child labor abuses while I have become preoccupied with creating employment. Her settlement house was situated in a crowded neighborhood composed mostly of immigrants from European countries. My city has experienced an exodus of biblical proportions and African-Americans make up the majority of the remaining residents. Addams dealt with the Industrial Revolution. I have struggled with the onslaught of information, the technological revolution and globalization. Jane Addams was awarded the Nobel Peace Prize and I operate a haunted house.

Still, I feel a kindred spirit with the reform leader. I gravitate toward Addams because she wasn't afraid to work at the grassroots level. She spent 36 years in Chicago's 19th Ward, most of it in tireless activity as if she understood that only a fraction of the things that cry out to be done can be accomplished in a lifetime even for those granted longevity. I hold her in high esteem because she was appalled by the injustice and indifference she witnessed. She reached the conclusion that poverty is complex but that its multifaceted nature is no excuse for failing to solve the toughest problems. Her bestselling book, *Twenty Years at Hull-House*, still provides a window through which to watch her personal development as well as the struggles and triumphs of her neighbors.

It is my hope that *Twenty Years at Cass Community* will install a window in much the same way. The short stories included are meant to reveal some of my incremental changes while they provide a fuller picture of the people of the community—their obstacles, foibles, tragedies, triumphs and tenacity. So often, poor people get reduced to numbers or graphs. When they are not treated like research data, they tend to be either vilified or regarded as helpless victims. One of my goals is to give a sense of them as three dimensional, flesh and blood people. A word of disclosure is needed though. Most of the names in the book are fictitious to protect the identities of those who wish to remain anonymous. A couple of the characters are actually composites, representing more than one person, because maintaining confidentiality required it.

I hope, too, that the book will capture some of the historically significant events that have transpired in the last 20 years. The O.J. Simpson verdict came down shortly before I started as pastor of Cass Church. During my tenure, we have collectively experienced 9/11, Hurricane Katrina, the election of Barack Obama, the Arab Spring, and mass shootings from Columbine High School to Sandy Hook Elementary. At the same time, as Thomas Friedman has observed, the introduction of technology has flattened the world. Twenty years ago, the Internet was surfed by only a handful of people. There was no social media—Facebook, YouTube, Twitter and Instagram all came after Y2K. People didn't Skype. No one had a smartphone. We used to take pictures with cameras and leave the film at the store to be developed and printed. We were still using beepers and scurrying to find pay phones 20 years ago. We rented movies from Blockbuster, not Netflix, and drivers unfolded huge paper maps without a GPS or Siri to direct them.

Like Addams' classic book, I expect that this one will serve as a time capsule of sorts, chronicling a particular period in southeastern Michigan. Two decades back, Detroit was a different place. The area has experienced a significant loss in population, political shifts and, of course, a financial crisis that pre-dated the national recession. In 2009, *TIME* issued a special report about these realities. The edition's cover superimposed bold white letters over a photo of the abandoned Packard plant which read, "The Tragedy of Detroit." What's more, the magazine purchased a house within the city limits for reporters, photographers and videographers to occupy for a year to further their coverage, not unlike the journalists who were embedded with the troops in Iraq. Michigan's governor appointed an Emergency Manager for Detroit and, within months, ours became the largest municipality in the country to file for bankruptcy in 2013. The impact was seismic. I have intentionally interspersed time and place sensitive information within the stories.

My *Twenty Years* book will also describe the evolution of the Cass organizations. It is important to note first that Cass Community United Methodist Church was involved in outreach and advocacy before I was born. Rev. John Perkins procured a pickup truck and used it for gleaning, thus starting the Cass food program during the Great Depression. Rev. Lew Redmond initiated programs for area children and seniors. He also established activities for adults with developmental disabilities during his 28-year appointment. Rev. Ed Rowe began the Homeless Drop-In Center, the Intra-Faith Rotating Shelter and the Free Saturday Clinic. When I arrived at Cass, all of these programs were going strong and all were under the church's administrative umbrella.

It became clear to me at the onset, though, that the neighborhood wanted fewer social services in the Cass Corridor and that the people needed more than emergency programs. Moreover, Cass Church had become the classic "tail wagging the dog." Every need and activity of the congregation was eclipsed by one of the social programs. Every inch of the church building was being used for supplies, food boxes, staff offices and meeting areas. Finding space for a funeral dinner or a youth group was problematic. So, we invited Lee and Jan Loichle to facilitate an exploratory team of congregation and program leaders to consider how we might reorganize Cass. At the conclusion of the sessions, the church voted to create a legally separate but linked nonprofit organization, naming it Cass Community Social Services (CCSS).

In 2002, in conjunction with the opening of the Scott Building four miles north of the church, CCSS was established. Since then, the nonprofit has grown exponentially. By 2013, the Food Program prepared and served a million meals annually. The Activity Center for Adults with Developmental Disabilities had increased to 125 participants, five days a week. In addition to the Warming Center and the Rotating Shelter, Cass added all of its transitional housing and permanent supportive housing so that 325 homeless men, women and children stay in one of our buildings every night. In response to the financial crisis, Cass began offering employment in 2007. Eighty-five permanent Green Industries jobs have been created and linked to sustainability. Finally, seven of the agency's 10 buildings are located within five blocks, establishing a pedestrian campus for residents, staff and volunteers.

The title of my book begins with a play on words from the African-American spiritual, "We've Come This Far by Faith." It is a reminder that the stories in this volume are from my viewpoint and my memory. I certainly didn't keep a journal or even notes. I have struggled over the years simply to record my mileage for the I.R.S. What's more, although other people were privy to most of the captured experiences, their recollections may not be the same as mine. Just as Moses' 12 spies returned from Canaan with two different reports, a person's perspective filters everything. Beyond this, I have tried not to interpret the stories for you. You must decide what they mean.

The 'this far' in both the song and my title implies that we have been on a long, often arduous journey and that we have made it to this point because God has been faithful, never failing us. It reminds us also that there is further to go. As long as poverty persists and opportunities are limited or denied, our work is unfinished.

Twenty-Year Timeline

Since the stories do not appear in exact chronological order, the timeline may help you have a sense of the sequence of events.

- 1994 – Rev. Fowler appointed to Cass Community United Methodist Church
- 1995 – Former Blood Bank building purchased
- 1996 – East Side Ministries taken over by Cass Community
- 1998 – Culinary arts classes began
- 1999 – Rev. Fowler purchased Corktown home
- 2000 – Warming Center started for homeless women and children
- 2002 – Cass Community Social Services nonprofit founded
- 2002 – Scott Building opened

- 2003 – Mom's Place I started for homeless women and children
- 2004 – Mom's Place II started for single homeless women
- 2005 – NFL at Cass Activity Center for Super Bowl XL
- 2006 – Warehouse purchased as distribution center
- 2007 – Rev. Fowler participated in White House Compassion in Action Roundtable
- 2007 – Residential Program opened for homeless men with HIV/AIDS
- 2008 – Green Industries replaced distribution center
- 2008 – Mom's Place I and II moved to Cass Campus
- 2011 – Brady Building purchased for permanent housing
- 2012 – Residential Program taken over for homeless women and children with HIV/AIDS
- 2012 – Wesley Apartments opened
- 2013 – Arthur Antisdel Apartments opened
- 2013 – Detroit filed for bankruptcy and CCSS Detainee Meals abruptly ended
- 2014 – Cass built a greenhouse

CHAPTER 1

Mental Health

"Hey Lady"

Undoubtedly, it was an omen. My first Sunday as Senior Pastor at Cass was a holiday weekend. No one was there. Even the associate pastor had deserted me for the Fourth of July. I stood alone in the impressive sanctuary that was built for over three hundred congregants. The loftiness of the ceilings only made the emptiness more exaggerated. Massive stained glass Tiffany windows and the immense 19th century Johnson tracker pipe organ were my only companions at five minutes to 11.

The choir finally filed in, just five people, including the accompanist/director. They stood around the grand piano and sang a few spirituals soulfully. As they performed, a dozen others began to drip into the sacred space. It was like a Chinese torture test. Each new person scattered into an empty pew, so as not to give the appearance of density. Probably 20 minutes into the service, a small group of adults with developmental disabilities arrived. They, I later learned, had been transported by the church van.

When it came time to deliver the sermon, I decided to pull out all the stops. Truth be told—any religious leader worth his or her salt wants to make a good impression that first time. We want people to leave the sanctuary, temple, mosque or auditorium overwhelmed by both our oratory and our spiritual depth. We want them to return for the next service with all the people they have told about our superior skills. It's hubris, I know.

Once I stood behind the ornate wooden pulpit in the center of the chancel, the numbers no longer mattered. I preached as if my life depended on it—employing expert exegesis, moving illustrations, memorable quotes and peppering the sermon with cadence and alliteration. We began doing the dance of call and response. Heads were bobbing and hands were clapping, in agreement, too. I became Howard Thurman and T.D. Jakes, Joyce Meyers and Bishop Judith Craig, John Wesley and Anna Howard Shaw. Just when I was about to burst into the burning bush, at the very rear of the room, standing directly under the doorway's thumbtacked exit sign, Harriett thundered at the top of her lungs, "Hey lady!"

I stopped mid-sentence, stunned. This had never happened to me before. In fact, I have since regularly suggested that people try it while they are on vacation to see if they can elicit a similar reaction from the resident clergy person. I lifted my eyes up off my manuscript as Harriett, age 62, developmentally disabled and a regular usher at Cass Church, completed her statement at an earsplitting volume, "We're out of toilet paper!"

I knew right then that I was in serious trouble. What do you do when all your academic training has left you unprepared for the work to which you have been called? I climbed out of the pulpit, found a roll of Charmin, and walked it back to Harriett. I realized in record time that she wasn't going to stop yelling until I did and that nothing I had to say would matter if I didn't.

"We've Been Robbed"

Not long after my arrival at Cass Community, Harriett got a new roommate. Many of the adults with developmental disabilities, who are connected to Cass, live in adult foster care (AFC) homes. Some of the homes were good—providing nutritious food and plenty of activities in addition to housing. Others homes were abysmal.

Harriett lived by herself in an apartment, enjoying her independence in a building with a homogenous population of about 40 residents. She occupied a two-bedroom unit, perfect for a couple of adults. Her new roommate, Ruby, was about the same age, and she, too, had a developmental disability. But that's where their similarities ended.

Almost immediately, I described them as an old married couple. It had nothing to do with sexuality. Rather, they complemented one another like hand and glove: Harriett walked while Ruby was confined to a wheelchair; Ruby could read and count, but Harriett was challenged by these skills; Harriett had a part-time job, but Ruby didn't work. What's more, Harriett was outgoing and cheerful while Ruby was introverted and cantankerous. She complained like most people breathe. But together, in tandem, their relationship worked. They formed an intense friendship and partnership.

The pair called me all the time—day, night, weekends, holidays. Often they just wanted to check on my whereabouts. Occasionally they had specific queries.

"Hello, Rev. Fowler, is it you?"

"Yeah, Harriett."

"Did you run the marathon?" she asked.

"I sure did," I said.

"Did you win?" she wanted to know.

"No, I didn't," I replied, without explaining that I just run behind the pack and that the winner from Ghana always crosses the finish line before I hit Wellesley College. In fact, the year in question was Boston's centennial marathon, and there were nearly 40,000 runners in front of me.

"Awe," she sighed, "that's too bad."

On another day, the phone rang and her voice was unrecognizable because she was in an absolute panic. "Revvvvvverrd Fowler," she stuttered, "weeee've been robbed."

"No!" I blurted out. "I'll be right over."

I jumped into my Cavalier and drove the mile to their complex. Once inside, I discovered that the crooks had followed the women home from the grocery store and knocked on the door while they were still unpacking their things.

Ruby opened the door and let them in. The bandits took small possessions—a jar of coins, some cheap jewelry and Harriett's answering machine. I told them that it would be all right—that everything could be replaced—that I was thankful that they weren't hurt but that I needed to talk to them about safety.

Harriett sank into the sofa and Ruby rolled her chair beside me. They were obviously still rattled by what had happened. I told them that the next time there was a knock on the door, they had to ask, "Who is it?" I asked if they understood me. Both heads nodded up and down and I had to remind myself that both women were old enough to be my mother (who of course had given me the same lecture years before).

I stayed long enough to know that they were okay and then I went back to work.

About a week later, the phone rang and it was Harriett. Her voice could have been a recording. "Revvvvvverrd Fowler," she stuttered, "weeee've been robbed."

What? How could this be? My mind raced. "I'll be right over," I heard myself say. Again, I jumped into my vehicle and made the trek to their apartment building. Again, I asked what had happened only to learn that there had been a knock on the door. "Did you ask who it was?" I demanded to know.

"Yes," they said in stereo.

"Well, what did they say?" I barked.

Harriett took the lead, "They didn't answer and so I opened the door to see." The crooks walked in for a second time and, like the first, they grabbed small trinkets worth a few bucks at most. I repeated my statement about how things could be replaced and the fact that they were unharmed mattered most. And then I went into lecture mode.

"Okay," I said. "When someone knocks on your door, you have to ask who it is. If they don't answer, don't open the door. If they tell you a name you don't know, don't open the door. If they say they are from some company, like the water company or electric company, or any other company, and you are not expecting them, don't open the door. If they tell you it's me and it doesn't sound like me, don't open the door … "

This last one was important because everyone in the neighborhood knew my name. Harriett and Ruby named their cat after me. Not Faith. Not Rev. Fowler. Rev. Faith E. Fowler. The two would let their cat outside and after a bit they would call for it to come back inside. "Rev. Faith E. Fowler, are you done going bathroom yet?"

I went through every possible human scenario in terms of who could be knocking on their door and when not to open it. And then again, I asked them, do you understand? Harriett had tears rolling down her cheeks as she confirmed her comprehension. I felt like I had just clubbed a baby seal. "Okay," I said, "I'll see you Sunday."

I succeeded at putting the episode out of my mind until the third week when the phone rang. Harriett was on the other end. "Revvvvvverd Fowler, weeee've been robbed."

I couldn't believe it. Maybe their building was just too dangerous. Maybe they needed a place with security staff. These thugs obviously had their number. The two were like sitting ducks. My car took me back to their apartment as if on auto-pilot.

The door was ajar and so I let myself in to the chaos of their apartment. They explained that they were watching TV when the knocking started. I interrupted Ruby, "Did you ask who it was?" "Yes," she said, feeling rather proud of herself.

"And, who was it?"

"They didn't answer!" Ruby again volunteered.

I exploded, "Then why did you open the door?"

"We didn't," she stopped. "They kicked it in."

I was speechless. Harriett began to sob. The same two men returned to the apartment and stole what wasn't theirs. They took a small radio and Ruby's purse. Then they rolled her into the bathroom and raped her.

Some of my more liberal friends object to talking about sin or evil. I don't. I know that people are capable of terrible things.

The three of us crowded into my compact car and drove to the hospital. The medical staff was kind to Ruby. After their examination and the necessary collection of evidence, I sat alone with her in the room. "Ruby," I said, "I want to call your dad. He'll want to know."

Bear in mind that many of the adults who come to Cass no longer have immediate family. Harriett's parents, for instance, were both killed in an auto accident, and she had no siblings and therefore no nieces or nephews. She is alone on the planet except for Ruby and the people at Cass. Ruby still had her father.

"No," she replied, "he won't come."

"Why not?" I asked. I thought she probably didn't realize how serious the incident was.

"He lives too far," came her answer.

"Where does he live?" I interrogated her, thinking that maybe he had retired to Florida or Arizona.

"Dearborn," she said.

Dearborn is a suburb 20 minutes from the hospital. She granted permission for me to call. I talked to him that afternoon. He never came.

Special Olympics

Adults with developmental disabilities are no different from other people in their love of sports. Many of the members at Cass have been involved with the Special Olympics for years, competing in track and field, softball, volleyball and basketball. One day, Sarah Lark, the program director, approached me about participating in a few new events.

"Don't you think we are offering enough?" I lamented in response. "What do you want to add?"

"Snowshoeing …" she said.

I had no idea that snowshoeing was even a sport. Chalk it up to city living, I guess.

She continued, "… and cheerleading."

Either Sarah didn't know that I'd done my graduate work at Boston University's School of Theology or she didn't understand the credos of progressive scholars. If BU ever learned that my church had a cheerleading squad, the faculty would undoubtedly demand the return of my diploma. "Absolutely not," I said emphatically.

Sarah was undeterred. "Come and see them," she said.

They were performing at a junior high school in Redford, an inner-ring suburb of Detroit. When I entered the gymnasium, they already occupied the center of the floor, dressed in uniforms that they had decorated themselves with glitter and their names on the back. Their shoelaces were neon glow-in-the-dark colors. The women were shaking pompoms as they cheered and chanted. At one point, the Cass squad even led the crowd in the Macarena.

"Oh my God," I blurted out loud, "I like them."

But I didn't like them because they were good. They were mediocre at best. I appreciated them because they had no loyalty. They cheered for both teams, which is how I think sports should be played, unless you're talking about the Lions.

Miss Cass

Once it was decided that we would keep the cheerleaders, the program director returned to plead for more. She said she wanted to establish a beauty pageant. That was the day we started drug testing our staff.

"Are you out of your ever-loving mind?" I thundered. "What a sexist, draconian suggestion. The whole world objectifies women and I will not be a part of it."

Sarah averted her eyes by looking down at her shoes, "They don't have any milestones, Rev. Fowler."

I mulled over her comment. Most men and women with developmental disabilities don't graduate from high school. Next to none learn to drive a car. It's rare for one of them to go to college, so they don't live in a dorm, join a fraternity or sorority, nor do they experience a spring break. Their families don't gather to watch them march to "Pomp and Circumstance" or listen to a graduation speaker discuss whatever ad nauseam. For the most part, they don't marry or have children. They don't land a dream job or get big promotions that involve a substantial pay raise or an office with windows. Men and women who are developmentally disabled never close on a house. They don't buy a cottage, plan a once-in-a-lifetime trip or spoil their grandchildren. Sarah was right. They miss out on celebrations. They don't receive the recognition that all people need and deserve.

"All right," I conceded, "you can have the beauty contest, but there better not be any swimsuits in my sanctuary."

The first step in the planning process involved soliciting the women on staff. Every female over the age of 12 has been asked at one point or another to stand up in someone's wedding—a family member's, a friend's, or a neighbor's. They go to a bridal salon and select floor-length gowns in some shade of Pepto-Bismol that makes each purchaser look like a sack of potatoes and costs a gazillion dollars. There are really no other options, in that all the other bridesmaids have to obtain identical dresses. They wear the gowns to the ceremony and the reception. Then they go to their respective homes and hang their dresses in their closets, where the formal wear will remain indefinitely. Where else would they wear those ugly dresses? Shopping at Kmart? Pumping gas at Sunoco? Out to the movies?

We had the women bring in their old outfits. We dry-cleaned them and tailored them and on the night of the Miss Cass pageant, 27 women sauntered down the center aisle of the church in their long dresses with hose and high heels, manicured fingernails, styled hair and professionally applied make-up. Each was escorted by one of the 10 gentlemen who were wearing tuxedos, none of whom had been invited to participate in anyone's wedding. Not one had even ever been a pallbearer.

In addition to being judged on the eveningwear, the female contestants performed individual talents. One led the audience in the *Pledge of Allegiance*. She remembered every word in order, even if she confused which hand to place over her heart. Another recited a poem that she had memorized. Jackie delivered *The Lord's Prayer*. After she finished, she added a knock-knock joke, thinking that it might help her win. A few women played musical instruments. There was plenty of singing, too.

Teddy-Bear Patty, who isn't developmentally disabled, but a senior citizen with Alzheimer's, surprised the attendees when she took center stage to croon. Patty is petite with salt-and-pepper hair and powerfully expressive brown eyes. Although she is amiable, her appearance is always disheveled. What's more, she doesn't have any teeth and her back is slightly hunched, calling attention to the fact that she is always holding something. Patty's nickname was given to her because, even though she has an apartment, she spends hours each day wandering the Cass Corridor streets, cradling a baby doll or a stuffed animal in her arms. When she opened her mouth to sing "Ave Maria" at the Miss Cass pageant, her perfectly pitched voice sounded like Adele and the crowd erupted with wild, effusive applause.

The majority of the contestants, though, preferred to dance. This wasn't a Fred Astaire and Ginger Rogers routine. The women became Tina Turner. The DJ started the musical numbers each contestant had pre-selected. One after another, they lit up the raised chancel "stage" and electrified the audience with their lip-synching, hand motions, footwork and sometimes overly suggestive body movements. Twirling, swaying, hip rolling, shimmying, even the splits were performed to Motown favorites and romantic classics. Sometimes it was hard to hear the music over all the cheering and clapping.

After the celebrity judges cast their votes for beauty and talent, the ballots were counted. There would be debate over the years about whether a winner should be chosen. I have always contended that part of our job is to prepare the women and men for real life and that real life includes sometimes winning and other times losing. All adults have to master how to deal with both situations.

A smaller group of finalists were selected to answer questions. The eight women stood poised in a single line on the stage, still in their evening attire. Last, they would be judged on their reasoning and personality. Even Vashti would have approved. Then the final votes were tabulated for the question-and-answer segment. A second runner-up and first runner-up were announced and, finally, Miss Cass was crowned. She stood, waving like Queen Elizabeth, before taking a final walk up and down the "runway" as the crowd applauded. The word 'crowd' was an exaggeration that first year. Only 15 or 16 people functioned as the audience. All of them were my relatives who owed me a favor.

Over the years, the audience swelled to more than 300 spectators. The popularity of the event can be attributed to a few things: just as many of the contestants and escorts lacked opportunities to be in the spotlight, their families and friends had gone without events that allowed them to publicly express their love, support and pride. Mothers and fathers began attending. Sisters and brothers, nephews and nieces started showing up. Cameras and video cameras were everywhere, recording their loved ones. The Miss Cass pageant provided the relatives a time to celebrate their accomplishments and talents. Staff and residents of their AFC homes came back year after year, too. They paid the five-dollar admission fee gladly. So did Cass employees, church members and volunteers who squeezed into the pews. Many of them knew first-hand how hard the participants have worked on their numbers.

Cass never even made so much as a flier to publicize the pageant, but more than once folks were willing to stand at the back of the sanctuary for the two-hour event because all 300 seats were taken.

It wasn't until the third year that we understood what the pageant meant to the contestants. That year our winner received her tiara before her adoring fans, and she refused to take it off. For nearly three weeks, it remained bobby-pinned to her head—she wore it to bed, in the shower, to shop and on the city buses. She wore it to church and to the Activity Center. She was Miss Cass and she wanted the world to know.

Slugger

The cover of the 2008 Annual Report is dominated by a photo from the final minutes of that year's Miss Cass pageant. The quality of the picture isn't the best because the lighting in the sanctuary is poor. But the content of the shot couldn't be any better.

Standing in a silky mauve gown with a red sash and her arms hoisted in a victory 'V' above her head is Betty. Her mouth is agape. Her title had just been announced, and the 300-person crowd was erupting in front of her.

Sixty-year-old Betty had secured her beauty queen status during the question-and-answer portion of the evening. Each of the final 10 contestants had selected a question from the emcee, Paula Tutman, a popular Detroit television news reporter. The questions were simple but caused the contestants to weigh their words and formulate their answers: What is your favorite animal? What is your favorite holiday? What movie do you like the best? What would you buy if you had extra spending money? How would you bring reunification to the Koreas? OK, so we didn't include the last question, but it makes about as much sense as some of the ones they use for televised pageants.

Each query was paired with, … *and why?* The second question gave both the celebrity judges and the audience a chance to hear how the women had arrived at their answers. Often the responses gave a glimpse into their thought processes and their life experiences.

Betty pulled an index card and Paula read the printed question, "What is your favorite song and why?" Betty stood mute and didn't respond. What the crowd didn't know was that Betty heard Paula ask her who was her favorite son. In fact, Betty was one of the only participants with children, all of whom were in the audience that night watching. How could anyone possibly admit to favoring one child above the others?

Paula repeated the question, unaware of Betty's dilemma. "What is your favorite song and why?" Everyone could sense that Betty was struggling. Finally, she burst out, "Bobby."

Bobby sprang up out of his seat like a jack-in-the-box jester. His siblings put two and two together almost immediately and they were none too pleased about his favored son status. The ruckus of the Betty's children helped the crowd slowly grasp the situation until their applause enveloped the room.

There would be no topping Betty's response. At the conclusion of the night, Paula Tutman announced Betty's name as Miss Cass 2008. Laura Beachum, the Cass board chair, stood ready to plant a sparkling crown on her head. Betty assumed the position of an Olympic champion, and then, right before the photographer snapped the picture that adorns our annual report, Sheila, one of the other finalists, raised her arm up to hit Betty.

Yep, Sheila hauled off and whacked Betty in the ribs instantly after the picture was taken. The photograph documents the instant before the slap. The shot perfectly captures Sheila's raw reaction. I've always thought that some of the runners-up in Miss America and Miss Universe would probably strangle the winner given the opportunity.

I love the photo because of what it says about Sheila. She was one of the first Miss Cass contestants. She had participated every year for a decade—learning dance routines, practicing jokes and performing magic. She altered her hair styles and dress colors in the hopes that a new twist would lead to victory. For 10 years she tried and for all of those years she lost. She was our own Susan Lucci.

Contrast that with the first decade of Sheila's life. She was just four years old when her parents dropped her off at a state mental hospital in Lapeer. I can't comprehend the depths of their pain, their conflict, their grief as they finally let go of all expectations they had for her.

I can't imagine being left behind in an institution before you could tie your shoes or spell your own name. What would it feel like saying goodbye to your family, your home and your pet? In an instant she was surrounded by strangers, professional and gentle though they may have been. Sheila's caregivers were there to work shifts. No one looked like her. No one was a blood relative.

Sheila spent the next 35 years of her life there. And then, the state decided that warehousing folks wasn't a very good idea. They deinstitutionalized people. For Sheila, that meant moving out with very few daily living skills and minus a family; her parents and siblings had relocated to Canada a few years after sending her away. It meant transitioning from an environment where everything was decided for her—when to get up, what to wear, what to eat, what to watch, how to handle hygiene—to a world rampant with scary choices.

The Miss Cass pageant had given Sheila confidence. Her decision to strike Betty made an indelible statement: I am talented, I am smart, I am pretty, I have worked hard and I deserve to win. To be sure, though, Sheila didn't win. Nor was she selected as Miss Congeniality or the recipient of the Mahatma Gandhi Award.

We told her story every time a 2008 Annual Report was distributed. The incident begged to be repeated. There she was on the cover in her green-with-envy evening gown, caught for eternity like Keats' young lovers in *Ode on a Grecian Urn*, with her fist about to deliver the blow to Betty.

At the 2009 pageant, the judges awarded Sheila the crown.

Going Up Yonder

It felt like I grew up in the back of a station wagon. My father was a teacher and so our family would use a few weeks of every summer to visit other states. That's probably why it shocks me that so many people never leave the city. It's especially true of poor people and those with disabilities. Thus, whenever possible, we organize excursions that will allow folks from Cass Community to experience the world beyond Eight Mile Road.

One of the annual traditions in Michigan is the Labor Day Bridge Walk. People come from both peninsulas to make the five-mile trek across the Mackinac Bridge from St. Ignace in Michigan's Upper Peninsula down to Mackinaw City, located at the tip of the Lower Peninsula. The walk is generally led by the current governor but involves an ocean of humanity— young and old, black and white, athletes and couch potatoes, families and singles.

I called the pastor of the Methodist church in Gaylord, four hours north of Detroit, and asked if he would allow a group from Cass to spend the night in his building. This would make the outing affordable. Rev. John Naile agreed to the arrangement, even though his congregation could have easily rented out the space during the holiday weekend. So, on the Sunday of Labor Day weekend, we loaded 50 adults with developmental disabilities and a few staff members plus volunteers into an old yellow school bus and made the journey up the I-75 expressway.

Everyone was excited about the prospect and even took to singing religious songs on the bus like "Breaking Up Is Hard to Do" and "99 Bottles of Beer on the Wall." When the vehicle finally pulled off the expressway, we stopped only briefly to pick up a couple of buckets of chicken and a handful of videos before settling in at the downtown church. There we unloaded, ate the fast food meal and arranged sleeping bags in rooms, segregated by gender.

Then we inserted the first video into the clunky church machine. Our travelers were mesmerized by each successive movie, which was probably good because they failed to notice how very hard the concrete floor was underneath their "beds." It was 2 a.m. before the last person dozed off to sleep.

Normally, the late night wouldn't have been a problem, but our early morning routine required extra time in a strange place—we got up at 4:30. The whole group had to shower, shave, dress, eat, brush their teeth, pack up their belongings and get onto the bus before the sun came up. The last leg of the journey took just about an hour. Still drowsy, the group managed to belt out a couple of verses of Michael Jackson's "Man in the Mirror" during the drive.

Mackinaw is a tourist town and never more so than for the Labor Day weekend. Bridge walkers swarm the city, packing the parking lots, streets, restaurants, hotels and gas stations. People flood into the staging area to wait for a bus to take them to the Upper Peninsula. The mob is ultimately forced into a temporary wood maze to wait their turns. Standing there with a few thousand people helps you understand the life of a cow. You stare at the rumps of the people in front of you while those behind must gaze at yours.

Our group was exceptionally good. No one complained of being bored. No one wandered away. Members engaged each other in polite conversation. A few were nervous, but no one asked to return home. We waited and waited and waited. All 50+ of us stood in line, inching slowly forward for an hour and a half.

Finally, when the first Cass walker was just four people shy of getting onto a bus, out of absolutely nowhere a worker emerged, cupped her hands around her mouth and bellowed, "The walk has been called off …. high winds." You've got to be kidding! What are we going to do, trapped with 40,000 tourists? We couldn't even get into a fudge shop and, if we could, how much fudge can you eat?

The group made its way to the water's edge. It was then that the women and men first realized that the suspension bridge hovered over water, and they were delighted not to walk. The staff noticed that the span was swaying visibly in the gale winds, and they were happy not to walk. It was only the second time since 1959 that the state called off the walk.

The return trip to Detroit was uneventful. There was no singing, but there was no crying either. I didn't think another thing about the excursion until April of the following year. My phone rang. It was Rev. Naile calling out of the blue. "Hey Faith, are you going to walk the bridge again?"

Now mind you, it was April. He was calling from a place that was as different from my setting as Mercury is from Mars. His congregation was situated in a lovely vacation town and there he was in April thinking about what a group of adults with disabilities in Detroit would do come fall. What was I going to say?

"Absolutely," I said. "Can we stay at Gaylord again?"

When Labor Day weekend rolled around, we were ready. After the worship service concluded, people packed back into the same ancient Cass bus. The group belted out the same contemporary "religious" songs. We stopped for chicken and videos, ate dinner at the Gaylord church, arranged sleeping bags on hard-as-rock floors, watched movies and talked until the wee hours in the morning. We rustled everyone up before the crack of dawn. They shaved, showered, dressed and ate … almost by rote.

Then, the staff presented a bright yellow rain jacket to every member of the group, just in case there was inclement weather. Group members boarded the bus, drove the final miles, dismounted and lined up like farm animals in the wooden maze. Everyone waited and waited and waited until we almost reached the fleet of school buses. And then, we got on.

There were audible expressions of awe and fear as the group rode over the "Mighty Mac." When we reached God's Country—people in upper Michigan refer to their peninsula as God's Country and they call folks from the south "trolls" because they live under the bridge—each person jumped down until everyone was assembled in a small crowd. The participants spoke in one unison surround sound voice. They all had to use the bathroom. Not a problem, the set-up was similar to the Boston Marathon. Rows of blue portable bathrooms were clustered together for those needing facilities. I issued instructions, since many of the members had never used a port-a-potty.

"OK," I said, "Here is what you do: stand in line. Wait your turn. When the person in front of you comes out of the bathroom, you go in. Lock the door. Do your business. Use the toilet paper. Don't worry about flushing or washing your hands. Then, unlock the door and come back here to me. I'll be waiting for you right here." I was slightly elevated on a grassy knoll.

They all scampered away, as quickly as cockroaches disappear when you flip the light switch in the middle of the night. I drank in the blue sky and cool, fresh morning air. I talked to a few tourists who approached me with questions. But mostly I watched and waited. The port-a-potty lines were 12 to 15 people deep, so I knew it would take a few minutes and I tried to be patient. I waited and waited. All by myself, I waited, when reminiscent of the woman who had announced the cancellation of the walk a year ago due to high winds, a state trooper appeared out of thin air and tapped me on the shoulder. "Ma'am," he said, "are those your people peeing in the woods?" Indeed. Evidently my directions were less than perfect.

When everyone was back, I attempted to do a better job describing how we were going to traverse the bridge. "OK everyone, you need to pick a buddy. We are going to use the buddy system like we do when we go swimming."

All paired up, I stood at the beginning of the group and took pictures as each team ascended the Mackinac Bridge. Click. Click. Click. Click. At the very end of our teams, Brenda was standing alone. I explained that I would be honored to be her partner, and, after a stranger took our picture, we began the five-mile walk together.

Walk is probably the wrong word. She was moving at glacial speed. It didn't matter, the fall weather was pleasant and the crowd was friendly. It wasn't a race, I reminded myself. We had time to talk. Everything was good until Brenda made her announcement. She turned to me and said, "Rev. Fowler, I have a leg cramp and I can't go any farther."

A good many people can tell you when they became a Christian. I can't. I was born into a church-going family. I was baptized as a baby alongside my three brothers and my father. My parents taught Sunday school classes and volunteered to assist the youth counselors. I have always believed in God. It's true that I have a few questions for God, but I have never doubted God's existence.

No, I can't tell you when I became a Christian. I can tell you when I became my mother. It was right there on that bridge. There were thousands of people behind us. There was absolutely nowhere to sit down. I was unaware of any shuttle service. Brenda weighed too much for me to carry her for the remaining four miles ... And so right then and there I morphed into Florence Fowler. I turned to my walking companion and without the slightest hesitation, I said, "Honey, we're almost there."

The two of us slugged across the gigantic span together. We met Elvis on the way. I took a Polaroid picture of Brenda as she received her certificate at the finish line. She held it in her hands like a Fabergé egg and grinned from her insides out. The snapshot and certificate went up on the refrigerator door the minute she got home. All these years later, they're still there.

The Human Jukebox

Over time, the number of adults participating in the programs at the Activity Center has increased from 40 to 125, and the average age of the people has significantly decreased. We opened up to young adults who can stay in school until they are 26 years old, but who desire educational, recreational and social activities during the summer. A sizeable number of the young adults of summer return the following season or permanently stay with our five-day-a-week program. Their life experiences and energy levels tend to be vastly different from the older adults, who spent years in institutions. The 20-somethings are generally more independent and social. The exception is the adults who have autism.

There is more than one type of autism and people can be affected mildly or severely. Men and women with autism can excel on college campuses and in corporate settings. Several of the people with autism at Cass have jobs. One works at a restaurant. Another is employed at a gas station. A third owns his own vending machine business through our supported employment program. Many more have sorting jobs in Cass' Green Industries. Typically, our adults with autism are nonverbal and they have difficulties when they are overly stimulated by their environment. One man spits at people indiscriminately and another secludes himself in a corner for long periods of time. The staff members at Cass patiently prompt them to learn new behaviors and to develop social relationships.

It's also true that many people with even the most severe autism have intense concentration capabilities. They can zero in on one thing and not be distracted. Jeremy can take a brand new 500- piece puzzle and, by himself, assemble it perfectly within an hour. Donald doesn't bother with puzzles, but he displays exceptional musical memory. He started at Cass when he was 18, after graduating from high school. Everyone knows that Donald can sing any song a cappella.

One day, Ed Hingelberg, our Director of Operations, spotted the dark-skinned young adult at a table and sat down with him. Donald was wearing his Tiger's baseball cap, and despite his serious demeanor, was quietly singing a succession of contemporary hits to himself. In his mid-50s, Ed was disheartened that he didn't recognize any of the current artists, and so he shared his frustration with Donald.

"How old are you?" Donald asked, as if Ed was a contemporary of George Washington.

Ed answered honestly.

Like a jukebox, Donald switched selections and began singing "Goodbye Yellow Brick Road."

"That's Elton John," Ed said, dumbfounded that Donald knew the words to a song that pre-dated Donald's birth.

"Do you know Sir Elton?" the singer asked with a knit brow.

"Not personally," Ed admitted.

Donald proceeded to sing lyrics from the Doors, Billy Joel and the Guess Who. His memory of the music was astonishing. Actually, it was doubly so in that Donald has never owned a record, cassette or CD. Donald has never seen sheet music nor has he even been to a concert. He had served as an escort for the Miss Cass pageant a couple of times. The year that Motown legend Martha Reeves served as one of the judges was his personal favorite. Donald has only a small radio in his bedroom. He listens to it in the afternoon and at night as he drifts off to sleep. Before offering to sing something from the Fab Four, Donald inquired whether Ed liked the old Beatles or the new ones.

"What's the difference?" Ed asked.

"The new Beatles sing songs like "Hey, Jude!" and the old ones sing "She Loves You.""

Around the block from Orchestra Hall, where the world-class Detroit Symphony Orchestra performs, Donald gave Ed a free music lesson.

East Side

Detroit is almost surgically separated into east and west by Woodward Avenue. Woodward stretches northwest from the Detroit River downtown all the way up through the suburbs until it dead-ends in Pontiac, a city of roughly 60,000, named after an 18th century Ottawa chief. Woodward Avenue is the center spoke of a wagon wheel of streets. The design was based on Washington D.C. and the capital's layout was modeled after the one in Paris.

Both sides of Detroit have been plagued with church closings during the last 50 years. Some of the congregations have merged and others have moved, but far too many have simply ceased to exist. The buildings are sold or sit empty. This is not to say that all the churches in Detroit have disappeared. There are a good number of vital ministries, including hundreds of storefront churches and a handful of thriving cathedrals, but church closings have played a part in the deterioration of the neighborhoods. Like removing tent stakes from the ground, without an adequate number of the anchors, a canvas structure or a local community collapses in on itself.

Sixty United Methodist city churches are gone. St. Mark's Methodist was eliminated in 1972, but unlike the closed churches, Richard wouldn't let it die. Who was Richard? An experienced clergy person? A lifetime pillar member? A wealthy benefactor? A community organizer? An area activist? No, Richard Kwiatkowski was the custodian at the eastside church.

Because he was the janitor, many were tempted to dismiss him. Without exception, Richard wore a military-style buzz cut, horn-rimmed glasses, and a pressed button-down shirt with cigarettes in the chest pocket. He generally rolled up his sleeves, exposing a Timex watch, and his shirt was always decorated with a green "Jesus Loves You" button. Richard was apt to give you a big bear hug, even if you were meeting him for the first time.

Congruent—that's what I call people like Richard. They are the same inside and outside, identical with poor folks and affluent people—what you see is who they are all the time. Richard began befriending the men and women who started coming to St. Mark's during the week. They lived in the AFC homes surrounding the steepled church. Some were put out during the day and others voluntarily escaped. The problem was that they had nowhere to go. They tended to be ignored or ridiculed and abused in the neighborhood. They were victims of crime and violence, so St. Mark's allowed them to come in and Richard offered them radical hospitality.

When St. Mark's closed its doors, Richard scrambled to find an alternative site for the weekday people. For about a year they shifted to a YMCA. Then, Richard convinced Bishop Loder to sell him the associate pastor's parsonage from St. Mark's for a dollar, so it could be used as a drop-in center. The two-story house on Hurlbut Street became a safe haven where adults from AFC homes enjoyed donuts, coffee with way too much sugar and cigarettes. They met there to assemble puzzles, watch television, to play cards and bingo. Five days a week, they came to the building to eat lunch and receive toiletries. A couple hundred participants would cram themselves into the downstairs living quarters for holiday parties.

East Side Ministries, as it became known, wasn't a church in the conventional sense. There wasn't a pulpit. There weren't any pews or hymnals or stained glass windows. God knows Richard never preached or took up a collection. In fact, he was always giving things away—food, clothes, magazines, bus tickets, hygiene products. When burglars constantly broke in to pilfer things, he would complain only that there was no need to steal because things were free for the taking. When Jesus told his disciples that they should surrender their coats if someone asked for their shirt and that they should walk a second mile, Richard took him literally.

The people at East Side didn't look like churchgoers either. They didn't arrive in "church clothes." They came casual and comfortable. Some were clad in tattered things, and a few wore three or four layers of clothing, even in the summer. These people never came by car. They walked the blocks between their group homes and East Side. They didn't worry about holding offices or nursing grudges the way that some people do in traditional churches.

Still, Richard rescued the mission of St. Mark's. He recognized that the people were at risk on the streets. The stores and restaurants threw them out like bags of garbage. Hoodlums physically attacked them for no particular reason. Crooks robbed them of what little they possessed. Richard created a sanctuary for a couple hundred mentally ill men and women, and he nurtured their community. To be sure, there were disruptive days when someone lashed out due to paranoia, irritation, depression, hallucinations … occasionally someone heard voices or suffered the side effects of their medication … but mainly they enjoyed a safe place to belong. The people called him Rev. Richard. He didn't have a diploma, a robe or a church building, but it was not lost on the people that his love was as unwavering as the green button on his shirt.

9/11

A phone call at 4 a.m. is never good. It was the next door neighbor. She told Richard that East Side was burning. When he arrived with his friend Melvin, the fire crew had already extinguished the flames, but they continued hosing down the first floor because smoke was billowing out the front door and the many broken windows. The smell of the charred building hung heavy in the air.

Initially they thought a burglar had accidently torched the old parsonage, but upon investigation it was discovered that the fire started with gasoline in the living room. It had been intentionally set by an arsonist. The blaze destroyed five rooms in total, including Richard's office. What wasn't badly burned suffered extensive smoke and water damage.

Richard was crushed. East Side Ministries closed. The people openly wept as they wandered the streets.

Fortunately, Mort Crim, a local news anchor, got wind of the situation and ran a feature story about the blaze. He was so moved by the tragedy that he sent a personal check to help with the rehab efforts. The local coverage brought volunteers from area churches to clean up the mess and begin the rebuilding process. They finished hanging new drywall and painting just in time for the annual Christmas party.

What's more, perfect strangers responded with financial donations. Their gifts, combined with the insurance money, amounted to enough to construct an entirely new activity room on the ground level at the rear of the house. Kip Serota, the brother of a Methodist pastor, worked with the famed architect Minoru Yamasaki. The two prepared architectural drawings for a great room, ideal for daily activities and spacious enough to accommodate 175 people during the holidays.

No one was thinking about the 1983 fire or the origin of the attached room years later, though. By then, the East Side Ministries board had finally accepted Richard's fourth request to retire after 23 years of service, and it had asked Cass Community to absorb the program. So, on that September morning, two Cass staff members were there—Gerald and Tasha. They were both in the large room, and it was packed with people drinking hot coffee, devouring day-old donuts and engaged in casual conversation.

"Did you see that?" Michael shouted.

Heads twisted and turned to look at what was then considered a big-screen TV. A collective gasp went out as they reacted to a replay of the passenger jet crashing into the World Trade Center tower. Like the rest of the nation, the members couldn't comprehend what was happening and they couldn't stop watching. People gawked at the television screen. Minutes later, the second plane slammed into the other tower and, as you know, after that the Twin Towers collapsed. While the news reporters talked about possible survivors and the courage of first responders, the clips of the two planes were rerun over and over as if they were on a Twilight Zone loop.

"How many buildings are they going to knock down?" Linda asked, disturbed and confused. She thought that each new rolling of the video involved another plane and another building. Gerald turned the television off before the hijackers hit the Pentagon and the passengers forced a crash landing of the fourth plane in Pennsylvania.

Yamasaki, who helped design the great room addition at East Side Ministries in which the television needed to be turned off, was the architect responsible for the World Trade Center, too. A second generation Japanese American, Minoru Yamasaki overcame the poverty and prejudice of his youth in Seattle but I am unsure if he could have recovered from the realities of 9/11. He had died in 1986.

XL

My mother taught me as a small child how to prepare the house for guests: dust, vacuum, clean and stock the bathroom and make the bed. Then, hide anything that remains unclean or out of place in the stove. The oven compartment is ample and able to conceal hundreds of items, if you stack them properly. It can accommodate books, boxes, dirty dishes, recycling containers, jars of change—almost anything can be packed inside so your house looks neat and tidy.

When it was announced that Detroit would be the host city for Super Bowl XL, many people worried that the city would use the stove trick with homeless people. It wouldn't involve a real kitchen appliance, but rather new ordinances and police sweeps. The purpose would be the same—hiding what we didn't want guests to see.

After multiple meetings with city officials and an intervention by author Mitch Albom, Detroit didn't repeat the mistakes of the 1996 Olympics in Atlanta, where thousands of homeless people were kept out of sight because they had been arrested or otherwise removed using one-way bus tickets. Nonprofit agencies across Detroit organized activities to include homeless people in the football festivities and to redirect the conversation about homelessness to include discussions about the urgent need for affordable housing, mental health services and living-wage jobs.

The stove in my Super Bowl experience had nothing to do with hiding people or things. It involved showcasing the work that was accomplished at the Cass Activity Center. Cass (CCSS) had been selected as the Super Bowl renovation project by Rebuilding Together, through the support of NFL Commissioner Paul Tagliabue and his wife, Chandler. Since the day after Thanksgiving 2004, hundreds of electricians, plumbers, painters, roofers, tile masons and carpenters had volunteered their time at the Activity Center. Some of the men and women were laid off. Others were paid by their companies to assist. A good number came from area churches, too.

What they did deserved the spotlight. They installed 5,250 square feet of new ceiling tiles, 79 new light fixtures, 1,400 square feet of vinyl flooring, 880 square feet of new carpeting and 20 new interior doors. They remodeled four bathrooms, applied 30 gallons of paint, replaced the front door and installed a new double door onto the parking lot for easy access. Finally, the tireless teams gave the program a new kitchen with a 16-foot counter, stainless steel sink with a garbage disposal, a dishwasher, and, of course, a beautiful new, empty-oven stove.

The official NFL Work Day was on February 3, 2005, two days before Pittsburgh would beat the Seattle Seahawks at Ford Field. The police and Secret Service-types were at Cass Church before 7 a.m. with bomb sniffing dogs. They needed to secure the church, the Activity Center and the high school across the street before the rest of the people arrived. A word of advice: Don't try and pet bomb-sniffing dogs. I was quickly chastised by an officer wearing an earpiece, that the K-9s were "at work" and I should not interfere with their search for explosives.

The heightened security was in fact necessary, in that all manner of dignitaries would attend the press conference about the Cass project that day. A few professional football players attended with the Tagliabues, as did Miss America. Local standouts included Roger Penske, Ralph Babb, Mayor Kwame Kilpatrick and his mother, U.S. Rep. Carolyn Cheeks-Kilpatrick, Rep. John Conyers, Sens. Carl Levin and Debbie Stabenaw and City Council President Ken Cockrell.

Two exchanges stand out from after the conclusion of the press conference. The first involved a former offensive lineman for the Lions, Lomas Brown. Six foot four inches and unnaturally wide, he was conspicuous when he walked into the Activity Center. After politely exchanging small talk with the electrical contractors from Union Local 58, he moved on to speak with a group of volunteers from Farmington Hills. One of the women, a senior, addressed Lomas. She said that she was a big fan and that she had followed him closely when he was in Detroit. All the while, the former offensive tackle had his hands buried in his pockets and he was smiling at her. Then the woman said that she was a little perturbed at him because he signed on with another team.

Lomas sheepishly said, "I'm sorry."

"I know what you got when you went down to Florida," she continued. "Can I see it?" Lomas lit up and pulled his hand out of his pocket.

"See it? Why don't you try it on and see if it fits?" he chuckled.

He handed her his 2002 gold and diamond-studded Super Bowl ring. She put the gigantic band on immediately. Her husband circled around the pair, scooted them together, placed his wife's hand on Lomas' shoulder so that the Tampa Bay championship ring could be seen. Then he started snapping pictures.

There were only finishing touches to complete on February 3, including the NFL Wall in the front meeting area. A staff member and celebrated artist, Vernard Rubens, had painted the Super Bowl logo on the wall. Celebrities, volunteers and participants from the Activity Center were to sign their names around the painting as a way of memorializing the event.

When one of our staff members was about to ask a couple of the children to please stay away from the dedicated wall, a Secret Service officer approached him and said that he might want to reconsider.

"This is a pretty important wall for us," the staffer said.

"Those are Rockefeller children," the officer responded.

Their painted handprints look lovely on our Super Bowl wall.

CHAPTER 2

Food

Leaving on a Jet Plane

"Tell him to sit down!" Vanessa Stewart squeezed my arm with the force of a mammogram. I looked up and didn't see anything out of the ordinary.

"Tell who to sit down?" I asked, puzzled.

"Him!" Her arm shot up as she spoke and her index finger extended like a laser pointer.

She had singled out the flight attendant. I didn't figure out what she meant, though, until my nervous companion began demanding to get off the plane.

"I want to get off! Tell him to stop the plane," and louder still, "I NEED TO GET OFF RIGHT NOW!" She was yelling. Heads pivoted in our direction.

Fifty-something, Vanessa had never flown before. She had only seen aircraft on TV and in the movies. Since the flight attendant was a man in uniform, she assumed that he was the pilot and that he had abandoned the cockpit while the jet was taxiing down the runway.

I started laughing uncontrollably, hysterically, as she completely cut off the blood supply in my arm.

I tried to think of a way to get her to relax. Ordering a Bloody Mary was out of the question. Vanessa Stewart was in recovery. You could never even get her to take an aspirin.

Slim and feisty, Vanessa came to Cass Community in the 1980s as a patient in the Cass Free Medical Clinic. Dr. George Costea, the clinic's founder and director, saw something beyond the scars on her arms and the ulcers on her legs. He made her a proposal. If she would complete a residential drug treatment program, Costea said that he would hire her to work at the Saturday clinic. Vanessa must have seen something in the doctor, too, because she admitted herself on his word alone.

I first met her four years after her stint in treatment. She was the picture of a Marine drill sergeant shouting out patient names at the receptionist's desk. Men and women came out of the gym waiting area and stood at attention in front of her. She grilled them about their medical history and captured their information using a pen and oversized white index cards.

The scene pre-dates HIPAA and nicely illustrates the need for privacy rights. "I have high blood pressure," one said. "I have sugar," said another using the street vernacular for diabetes. He was missing a foot. Even those with sexually transmitted diseases reported to Vanessa right out loud.

"The truth don't need no support," Vanessa would say, meaning that we should be transparent. She had learned that lesson in rehab with the Salvation Army and, like most new converts, she was a fiery evangelist for God and sobriety.

I hired Vanessa to work during the week because I saw something in her, too. I'm also convinced that people with similar experiences can both encourage one another and hold each other accountable in ways that elude people without that experiential glue. She started in the Homeless Drop-In Center, then shifted to become the manager of our emergency food program.

Vanessa and I were on the departing airplane together because we were on our way to visit the D.C. Kitchen. A Ted Koppel *Nightline* episode had piqued my curiosity about Robert Egger's entrepreneurial nonprofit in the nation's capital. I was convinced that seeing his food-rescuing, job-training and meal-serving operation would spur us to think about ways to eradicate hunger in Detroit. After all, Cass had been feeding people since it established a soup kitchen during the Great Depression. For over 40 years, thousands of people had stood in line with downcast eyes, outstretched hands and empty plates. Thousands of volunteers had worked in the steaming hot kitchen, performing magic on stainless-steel counters with dull knives and donated produce. Thousands of dollars had been granted and given to purchase food and pay a small but dedicated staff. What difference had it made? I had begun to ask what difference another forty years of serving would make and whether we were dishing out a little dependency with every meal.

Our plane landed smoothly, but you would never know it from the imprint of Vanessa's fingers on my upper arm. After retrieving our luggage, we caught a cab to the kitchen. We walked down a back alley and past several box trucks parked in the loading dock before entering the basement of a homeless shelter. At first it seemed like an odd environment for innovation. Once we were inside, though, ideas started flying around in my head like paper airplanes in a fourth-grade classroom. Everywhere I looked there was someone or something I wanted to imitate, replicate or modify for Cass. Vanessa caught the fever, too. She even said she was glad she had gone once we were back home.

It took us a year, but Cass created a culinary arts program loosely modeled after the 12-week curriculum at the D. C. Kitchen. It was the beginning of the change for which I had hungered.

Two Things

Picture the chef at an upscale restaurant, impeccably dressed in baggy black and white houndstooth pants, a crisp white chef coat and a matching white toque. That was the graduation garb for the Cass culinary arts students. Each matriculating member of the class marched into the sanctuary, single file down the sloping center aisle, in front of their applauding spouses, children and parents.

Fourteen anxious and elated men and women took their seats of honor in the front two pews. New students about to begin the intensive 12-week culinary training program sat in the next section over, absorbing the excitement of the morning.

Grace Bailey took the microphone first. She described the strict requirements of the vocational course:

"You see that not everyone who started the classes is here. Thirty students received ServSafe manuals 12 weeks ago and only 14 will receive diplomas today. You are to be congratulated. You learned the lessons.

"You have to show up, on time, every day," she said hoping that it would sink in for the newest students. "It doesn't matter if you are tired. We don't care if you missed the bus. If you are on time ... "

"You're late!" The graduating class finished the speaker's mantra.

Next up was Chandra, affectionately known by everyone as "Shorty" because she's only 4 feet 11inches tall. She climbed up on top of an upside-down plastic milk crate behind the pulpit podium. Talking a frantic pace reminiscent of "Flight of the Bumblebee," Shorty reviewed some of the health and safety materials. "I know you won't forget how important it is to monitor food temperatures, rotate stock, segregate cutting boards, cover your hair and wash your hands. Let me say it one more time: wash your hands and then put on some gloves!"

She went on at her rapid tempo, and the students seemed to be reviewing the lessons they had learned from the daily readings and from the mistakes they had made in the kitchen. Just a short while ago, they were unaware that hands should never be used in place of an ice scoop or that a spoon could only stir one dish type before it needed to be washed. The smokers had required constant reminders initially about removing their aprons and gloves before they went outside, and washing their hands again before resuming their activities. Most had to learn about the precautions now required for a dozen different food allergies. Shorty's son, William, was allergic to dairy products as well as pork, chicken, turkey, fish, peanuts and a boatload of vegetables.

In time, the crowd grew restless. People were ready to move on to the distribution of diplomas and the announcement of the class valedictorian. Since the students didn't receive grades, the person with the highest score on the ServSafe test was deemed valedictorian and invited to deliver a farewell speech during the ceremony.

Cass cook Joe Martin disclosed the winner.

Joe had learned to cook at Ft. Leavenworth in the 1970s. Tall, quiet and gentle, he had battled his own addiction demons over the years. He caused an auto accident while he was under the influence of alcohol, and the threat of prison time finally helped him rearrange his priorities.

"I am pleased to announce that all 14 of our graduates passed the ServSafe exam and Delores had the highest score with a 96 percent." The room erupted as if Detroit had been selected as the site for the next Olympic Games. Graduates jumped to their feet in order to exchange high fives and hugs.

Delores began her comments by saying that she hadn't prepared anything. Nevertheless, she certainly could have guessed that she was a contender. In her late 30s, Delores was a quick study. "You know that my children are here," she said with tears streaming down her checks. Her classmates and teachers knew that her kids had been taken from her and that she had feared that they would be blocked from attending the ceremony.

"I'm so glad they are here to see me get my diploma. Until today, I never finished anything. I quit high school. I ran away from home. I walked away from my marriage. I got fired more times than I can count. About the only thing I didn't quit was drinking. Then, I lost you and I lost my mind."

She had to take a moment to compose herself because her voice began to crack.

Delores held her hand up as if to say, *give me a minute.* Individual classmates called out to encourage her: "It's all right." "Take your time." "You did it."

"I was determined that I would finish this class," she said. "It wasn't easy … but I did it. We did it and no one can take that away from us."

Just before the diplomas were handed out, the graduation ceremony had a keynote address. Generally a local luminary talks, but on this particular day the celebrity speaker canceled at the last minute. We asked Alan Murphy, a case manager from the PATH program, to pinch-hit.

Alan was decked out in a loud yellow suit and brown tie. He was short in stature but a giant in the community. He addressed the house without resorting to notes.

"When I was homeless, I stayed in a cardboard box on Second Street," Alan began.

"Some days I would go into Tom Boy Market and steal packaged lunch meat. It was easy to tuck it into the waist of my pants. When I got back to the corrugated shelter, I always wished that I had some mayonnaise to go on the meat, but the condiments were too close to the counter and I didn't want to get arrested.

"It's a funny thing, when I was in prison, I missed having the box. It had offered me privacy and a sense of security. I kept a few small personal things inside. While I was incarcerated, nothing was safe even though there were locks everywhere. I didn't have any keys.

"If you came to my house today, you'd find more than one bottle of mayo in the refrigerator."

Alan reached into his pants pocket and pulled out a ring full of keys.

He lifted them up for everyone to see. "And here are the keys to my house, my car, my office, my mailbox and my bicycle lock," he said.

"Congratulations on your achievements. Don't ever take the small stuff for granted. You must determine the two or three things that you really want and then go get them."

Alan Murphy hit the ball out of the park.

Food for Thought

I shop for groceries at 7-Eleven. The lines are short and you never have to use a scanning machine to check yourself out. It's not as hard as you might think because I have only two food groups: chocolate and Diet Coke.

After watching Robert Billings eat at Cass for a few months, I came to the conclusion he only had two food groups as well. It doesn't matter if you use the food pyramid or the current sectional dietary plate; Robert eats hot sauce and everything else. More accurately, he pours hot sauce on everything else—meat, fries, potato chips, popcorn, eggs, cereal and gum. Nothing goes into his mouth without a couple squirts of the reddish-orange sauce. No sugar, no salt, butter, sour cream, whipped cream … No problem. No hot sauce … Stop the prayer. Put down your fork. The meal will have to wait until someone can run to the neighbor's or the store.

Like countless people at Cass, Robert was raised in the South. He grew up in rural Alabama. Cass Community southerners not from the Yellow Hammer State spent their formative years in Arkansas, Mississippi, Louisiana or Georgia. A few hailed from cities in Florida but far more lived in the farm communities of the other states. Thus, many people who are a part of Cass have a preference for southern cuisine.

I didn't think much about food choices until I overheard a homeless person one day refer to a meal as "white" food. Surely you have to always be cautious about lumping any group of people together, but in that instant I was reminded that race and class and religion and geography all play into what we devour.

"Hey, Robert," I stopped him on his way out the door one afternoon. "If you were in charge of the menu for Thanksgiving, what would we serve?"

"If I could have anything … " You could see his mind engage, as he rattled out his choices, a smile began to dominate his face. "I'd have ham and turkey, macaroni and cheese, yams, greens, black eyed peas, corn bread, dressing and pie … sweet potato pie."

I was surprised he didn't mention hot sauce. He probably thought I knew that it was a given. His recommendations caused me to think about what I would have proposed for the holiday. I undoubtedly would have recited the things that were a tradition in my family—lumpy mashed potatoes and gravy, cranberry sauce, warm dinner rolls, deviled eggs prepared by the youngest children, turkey that had gone into the oven before we headed down to the Hudson's Thanksgiving Day Parade, stuffing, classic green bean casserole and pumpkin pie. Our family was generally and woefully divided between whipped cream and Cool Whip.

How different the items on Robert's list were, yet how we determined the items was very much the same. Food preferences are first taught to you by your family and the community in which you are raised. Did your father hunt? Did your family fish? Was your mother always on a diet? Did your pet get the table scraps or were the leftovers wrapped up for the next day? Did you go out to restaurants to eat? Did your family go to the farmer's market or did you have a garden or live on a farm? Did you have to sit at the table until your plate was clean or listen to an elder scold you about the hungry children in India? Did your people try dishes from other cultures? Did your parents let you experiment with food selections?

I remember telling my mother that I was done eating meat at age five because my older brother had graphically described the origins of a hot dog to me. An animal lover, I was ready to join PETA on the spot. My mother never forced the issue, and from that day until this one, the only things I consume that used to have eyes are potatoes. Food is as much about memories and emotions as it is about nutrition.

The Cass staff let me plan the menu for that Thanksgiving and every one since then. (Normally I don't get a say in the kitchen because everyone knows that I don't cook.) I made sure that several of Robert's suggestions were included—yams without marshmallows, greens without pork, sweet potato pie without whipped cream, and macaroni and cheese with everything but the kitchen sink.

Mac 'n' cheese was one of the few dishes I made while I was in seminary. It was cheap, less than a dollar a box at 7-Eleven. It was easy. You just have to know how to boil water and drop in the elbow noodles and the bright orange powder with a little margarine. But for Thanksgiving at Cass, I learned what a different dish it is when prepared southern, soul-food style. Our volunteers bake the macaroni dish with three or four kinds of cheese. Eggs, milk and butter are mixed in so that the pasta dish is heavy, like quiche loaded with meats and vegetables. Robert makes his "perfect" by smothering it all with hot sauce.

Volunteers handle everything for the Thanksgiving feast. On Thanksgiving eve, about 20 adults head to the church after their annual Gratitude Meeting. These members of Alcoholics Anonymous and Narcotics Anonymous scrub down the windows, chairs and counters. They sweep and mop all the floors, and then they assemble in the kitchen to wash several hundred dishes. Thanksgiving is the only day of the year at Cass that people eat off china plates on top of linen tablecloths.

When the night team is done preparing the tableware, they move on to the turkeys. Forty roasted turkeys have to be pulled apart and organized into warming trays. Bones in one pile, legs in another. White meat and dark meat gets separated. Scraps go into a pot for gravy and the necks and internal organs end up in another for those who ... This is not a task for a vegetarian, so I'll let you imagine the rest.

Early in the morning, around 6 a.m., 60 teenagers and their chaperones arrive from Renaissance Baptist Church. They prepare a breakfast fit for lumberjacks and serve it to people staying in our shelters. They also begin the lengthy process of chopping up vegetables for cooking and for dipping—celery, carrots, onions, green peppers, cauliflower, cucumbers, lettuce, tomatoes and potatoes. The crew from Renaissance Baptist have been coming for so many years that they bring their own knives and peelers.

When they are finished, individual volunteers and families arrive to finish preparing the meal. By then, eight or 10 huge pots are sitting on the commercial oven's eyes. The gas flames are leaping up and licking the bottoms of the metal containers. The only thing more fragrant than the fresh cut flowers on the tables is the aroma of turkey and ham nearly finished in the oven. Bonnie Christler and her family direct the volunteers so not a minute is lost. There are sweet potato, pecan and pumpkin pies to be cut.

As the guests arrive, we remind them that this meal will be different from the ones they had as children because we try to include as many traditions as we have groups of people. I joke that no one will have to sit at a card table. The meal is different from most other days at Cass, as well. There is no need to stand in a line. They can select a seat at a table of their choosing. The volunteers will bring serving dishes to them, loaded with food made from scratch. Each person can have as little or as much as they like of any item. We will gladly refill the china dishes until everyone is full. Don't feel the rush to get up so someone else can have your seat, I tell the guests, who by this time are packed into the church gymnasium. On Thanksgiving, it's about companionship and comfort food. We hope you have a voracious appetite.

God Bless Us, Everyone

For over 20 years, Christmas at Cass has included the good people from the Saline United Methodist Church. From an hour away, they arrive like a flash mob with decorations, dinner and presents divided among 20 cars. Jim O'Kunze was in charge of the annual affair when I started at the church, but he retired and moved to Florida after just a few years. With such an energetic and capable leader gone, I feared that the relationship between the churches might fizzle out and that this rare celebration given to the Cass Community might be lost.

Lucky for us, Jim had tapped "B" (Bonnie) and Carlos Melendez to carry on the holiday tradition. B, a nurse by trade, was highly organized and automatically assembled lists and coordinated the 60 or 70 church volunteers with the ease of a computer database. This included her own young children, Alexandra, known affectionately by everyone as "Bug," and her older brother, Francisco, AKA "Frisco."

When the group arrived at Cass, Bug initially worked the treat bag assembly line with her mother. Three eight-foot tables were pushed together to lay out the snacks. People would walk from one end to the other, picking up 12 different homemade cookies, a piece of fresh fruit as well as a candy cane and put them in Ziploc bags to be distributed with the gift packages as people left the building after eating. It didn't take long for Bug to be promoted to treat-bag leader, showing others how to amass the giveaway goodies.

Once the finished bags were tucked away, Bug would move on to assisting with the table setting, putting out decorated placemats, plates, cups, silverware and colorful napkins before adding scented Christmas pine cone arrangements.

After the 11 a.m. worship service, Bug changed jobs once more. B made her young daughter a "greeter and seater." This assignment seemed slightly unfair to me. Bug was a very quiet, introverted, sensitive girl. She appeared uncomfortable in her own skin, even when talking with her own family. What's more, she was anything but demonstrative. Bug demanded an inordinate amount of personal space, and some of the folks at Cass don't know what personal space is. It was a recipe for disaster, but for all of her daughter's protests B didn't let up.

Frisco tried to help. He'd deflect a few of the 6-footers who insisted on bear-hugging his much smaller sister, but he couldn't catch every person who approached. It was there, in the entrance to the gym, serving like a Walmart greeter, that Bug encountered Teddy in 1994. She was 11 and he was a young adult with developmental disabilities. He caught her by surprise and scooped her up in his arms. In fact, at first, she was unsure if he was a man or a woman. Her head was smashed against his thick winter jacket. She tried to gently dislodge herself from his embrace, but he held her tight. He actually began to squeeze her small frame as he hugged her.

Eventually, Teddy released her. She wasn't harmed. The incident probably helped her slightly to overcome her physical aloofness. Asking around, Bug learned that Teddy lived in a group home and that, like so many people, he was starving for, intensely craving, human touch.

The two would see one another occasionally when the Melendez family worshipped at Cass, and by the next year, Teddy stood with Bug at the door to welcome others into the gym. It was funny to watch, in that the job Bug had found so disconcerting became a prize that she was determined not to relinquish to Teddy. He wasn't looking to replace her. Teddy just wanted to be close to her. He had an obvious fondness for her. He would talk incessantly, asking her a billion questions, and Bug would respond with one-word answers while darting looks at her mother across the room. Bonnie was shooting looks back that said, "You'd better be kind." Finally, the allure of food would take over, and Teddy would join the crowd for Christmas dinner.

He first proposed when Bug was 13. He had tracked her down and sat next to her in a pew. Half the church from Saline was watching them instead of paying attention to the service. As always, he was blubbering on a mile a minute and Bug was only half listening. Then, she heard him pop the question, "Will you marry me?" She was thoroughly mortified. Bug became obsessed with ditching him for the next year.

Nevertheless, every Christmas after that one, he waited for her to return, and slowly Bug started looking forward to catching up with Teddy. The hugging part still put her ill at ease. Yet, as she grew older, his clinch no longer scared Bug. Nor did his annual request for her hand in marriage. Her responses came more easily. Bug actually began to feel flattered that he had singled her out. She no longer even minded Teddy's help seating the Christmas guests. The unofficial couple started playfully bantering back and forth.

When Bug was in college, Teddy decided to add an enticement, since Bug kept rejecting his proposals. He told her he could give her a car if she married him. She asked to see the vehicle, and he reached into his chest pocket and plucked out a red Matchbox convertible. He was proud of it. Bug was sensitive to his feelings and complimented him on the sports car. When Bug told me the story, I pointed out that most of her college dates couldn't provide her with a car and that I was available for pre-marital counseling.

When Noah, her college boyfriend, proposed to Bug, she said she realized that she must have been the first, possibly the only female Teddy had asked to be his fiancé.

"Teddy is such a loving soul. I'm glad I got to know him. He became a part of my Christmas. His proposals were a gift."

Now Bug's veterinarian husband, Noah, accompanies her to Cass on Christmas Day. Teddy no longer proposes; maybe he comprehends that she is married. Bug has observed that he now eats with a special friend from the neighborhood. It gives her sheer joy, but she has also confided that there is a part of her that is disappointed. Her relationship with Teddy has become distant. I suspect that if he surprised her one holiday with a close embrace, Noah wouldn't be jealous and Bug wouldn't mind that Teddy had invaded her space.

The best Christmas gift exchanges tend to be reciprocal.

Takeaway Meals

The health department has strict rules about where you can eat the meals made in a commercial kitchen. Mostly the rules protect the temperature of the food because if it becomes too hot or too cold, you run the risk of bacteria making people sick. The majority of our meals are served at one of our sites, but there have been a few exceptions.

When a new veterans residential program was ready to open, the commercial kitchen was unfinished. The group's deputy director called and asked if we could prepare and deliver three meals a day to the facility for a couple of months. It was a no-brainer. We certainly had the capacity and I have always felt that no matter where you stand on war, there is only one place to be in relation to the men and women who put themselves in harm's way. We must stand with them. Thus, for three years, we made breakfast, lunch and dinner in the Cass Church kitchen and dropped the meals off at the Vets Center. "During the blackout of 2003, which began in Ohio and cascaded throughout the Midwest and Northeast, and even to parts of Canada, Cass prepared meals without electricity or fans. In the August heat and humidity for four consecutive days, food staff member Karl Martin loaded the covered pans onto a chrome utility cart. He pushed the cart, stacked high with pans, serving spoons, paper products and beverages, down Cass Avenue for eight blocks so that the homeless veterans wouldn't miss a meal.

Cass has provided similar congregant meals to a hospital, some charter schools and for several summer lunch programs. Each of these arrangements was for just a year or two at a time.

For over a decade, we did home delivered meals—Meals on Wheels—for homebound seniors living in 13 different ZIP codes. Early on, I joined Frank Pearson, the delivery staff person, to conduct my own little satisfaction survey. Did the people like the meals? Was the hot food hot and were the cold dishes cold? Did the dishes look good? Did the food taste good? Was there enough variety? How about the portion size? And, what about the staff—were they polite and friendly, did they arrive on time?

Although Detroit has been a city filled with single-family homes, unlike New York or Chicago, most of our stops were at apartment buildings. I'd climb the steps or use the elevator to reach an apartment and then talk with each person for five or 10 minutes. It didn't appear that the seniors minded the interruption. Their feedback was helpful and overwhelmingly positive.

Then, the Cass driver pulled up in front of a bar. "What are we doing here?" I asked him.

"We're dropping off a meal."

"What?" I thought I had heard him wrong.

"Yeah, Rev. Fowler. We drop off a meal here every day for Mr. Budd."

"We do what?" I was sure Frank didn't know the Methodist Church's historic stance on alcohol.

The driver read my nonverbal cues and said, "You don't understand Rev. Fowler. Mr. Budd doesn't drink."

"Right," I responded, meaning *do you think I just fell off a turnip truck?*

"No, Mr. Budd doesn't drink. His wife died seven months ago and he just can't bear to eat alone."

Some of the take-out meals are about nutrition, and some aren't. The vast majority of the meal recipients are poor, but they also struggle with shopping, cooking and cleaning. Most are terrified that one day they will fall and break an arm, a hip or a leg. These seniors worry that no one will know that they are hurt, so they are grateful for the men and women from Cass that stop by each day. Frank even took out the garbage for a few seniors. At one apartment, he changed a light bulb. At another location, he chatted with someone a little longer because it was the man's 84th birthday. Everyone received food, but so much more was taking place.

Conversely, other Cass takeaway meals are all about food. In 2001, the U.S. Justice Department demanded that Detroit put detainee meals out for bid. I obtained the Request for Proposal. It explained that the Detroit Police Department needed a food service vendor in order to feed people who were locked up in the precincts. I called the contact number provided at the bottom of the notice.

"I'm sorry," I said. "I've never been arrested. What do you serve?"

"Sandwiches," came the reply.

"OK. And how about dinner?"

"Sandwiches," he said.

"And breakfast?"

"Sandwiches." The sergeant wasn't much of a talker.

We can do that, I thought. Anyone can make a sandwich. Our development team worked through all of the requirements, including securing a bid bond, which ultimately meant that I would lose all my worldly possessions—house, car, cash and dog—if we ever failed to deliver a meal. The voluminous application was submitted and Cass won the competitive contract. On the day before the contract began, Cass didn't make a single sandwich; on the next day, Cass prepared and packaged 1,200.

It's a good thing that those early weeks predate YouTube. The so-called meals were taken to 13 precincts each night, and the next day we'd start again. The kitchen crew eventually became experts in stacking sandwiches to make them. We churned out ham, turkey, and salami with cheese as well as peanut butter and jelly. As you might expect, the PB&J sandwiches were the worst to prepare. Jelly, although it smells wonderful, adheres to a sandwich maker's gloves, apron and hat. The countertops become purple. Even a person's shoes act like jelly magnets. Everything becomes sticky and gross.

Our thought was that the detainee meal program could have a triple impact. First, we could use the program to provide vocational training for people interested in culinary arts. Although making sandwiches is simple and repetitive, trainees would have to be able to follow directions, stand on their feet for extended periods of time and learn the basics of food safety. Second, the detainee meal program would generate a little revenue for the other food services that weren't adequately funded. And third, but equally important, delivering detainee meals would put us in every police precinct every night.

Being known by the police is critical in a big city, especially when you are dealing with situations that require rapid response time. The police are spread thin, particularly at night, and the officers are paid poorly. It is not uncommon to call and wait for hours for assistance. With some scenarios, they don't respond at all. If your car is involved in an accident, they tell you to come to the station. If someone is stealing your car battery or rims, the cops are preoccupied with bigger, more violent crimes. We needed the police to know who we were so they would respond when there was a critical incident at Cass. In addition to the sandwiches, our driver would sporadically leave treats for the officers—brownies or cookies; a tray or a hot meal for the holidays.

When the City of Detroit declared bankruptcy in 2013, the 11-year detainee meal contract was terminated. Heaven knows what the prisoners are eating now.

Urban Gardens

With so many vacant lots in Detroit and the scarcity of grocery stores, urban gardens have become as common as bulletproof glass in the area's gas stations. Many gardens are small and tended by a single family or two. Community gardens can be as large as a city block and managed by scores of neighbors or a nonprofit. The spectacular thing about the city gardens is that they bring together the issues involved in food justice and food safety. City dwellers gain access to fresh, relatively free, and mostly organic vegetables because of the gardens.

Gardens aren't universally regarded as something positive though. You can blame it on the Bible. Hebrew Scripture begins with "the Garden." Adam and Eve ended up in trouble in Eden and God decided that agricultural undertakings would be difficult for Adam thereafter. The New Testament Garden of Gethsemane is where Jesus, overwhelmed to the point of sweating drops of blood, went to pray to ask God for another outcome.

Personally, I was opposed to gardening because I prefer people to plants. I like my species. I never wanted to be surrounded by corn or carrots, cows or composting. Maybe it is because I had to pull weeds with a knife every summer as a kid. My father expected us to eliminate 25 dandelions a day and if you didn't get the roots, it didn't count toward the tally.

The only thing I dislike more from my childhood is camping, but that's another story.

Against all my better judgment, Cass decided to establish a few gardens. We tested the soil, and then started growing tomatoes, onions, cucumbers, lettuce, radishes, squash and spinach. One of our volunteers even taught us how to use a drip irrigation system so that the gardens would use only a small amount of water.

One day, when a team of interns and volunteers were planting on an empty lot, a man from the community hollered at them as he walked down the street,

"So we are going back to the plantation!"

Some resistance falls along color lines.

After Cass had 10 productive gardens, the staff started thinking about how we could better utilize the land. The answer was potatoes. Potatoes are the perfect crop for Michigan. They don't require additional water. Rainwater is adequate. Potatoes are a root plant, so people and critters won't bother the food. And, probably most importantly, potatoes don't spoil the way other vegetables do. You can store them from September until April, as long as you keep them somewhere dark and cool. Finally, even beginning cooks can serve potatoes countless ways—mashed or baked; as French fries or hash browns; in potato salad and potato soup ...

Still, one vegetable wasn't enough to feed folks throughout the year. The thing about hunger is that people are just as hungry in November and March as they are in June through September. We considered canning but there wasn't sufficient storage space. Then we evaluated adding a hoop house. The staff worried about the durability of a plastic covering. Ultimately, we decided that we wanted to extend the growing season to a full 12 months. What we needed was a greenhouse.

I called my niece. My middle brother had moved to a farm about 60 miles outside Detroit because his wife loved gardening and horses and he loved his wife. Their daughter and my niece, Melissa, grew up on the farm raising rabbits, goats and pigs to show at the county fair. She earned a degree from Michigan State University, married a farmer and today teaches 4-H at a high school about 125 miles from Detroit.

"We're thinking about putting up a greenhouse to grow food hydroponically all year," I told Melissa. "What can you tell me about setting up a greenhouse?"

"Have you called the police?" she asked.

"Why would I call the police?" I asked, thinking I should check in on her more regularly.

"They can donate the lighting and accessories from their drug raids." There she was, living in the "thumb" of Michigan's "mitten," with its gently rolling topography, mile after mile of grain, beans, sugar beets and barns, telling me about raiding illegal drug operations. Next she'll be teaching me about graffiti and gangs.

CHAPTER 3

Homelessness

Den of Thieves

Holman Hunt's famous painting of Christ is displayed in nearly every Protestant church built before 1965. The reproduction portrays Jesus knocking on a closed wooden door. Upon inspection, you realize that there is no door handle. Thus, it must be opened from the inside. The symbolism is that Jesus waits to be invited in to a person's heart. I know better. The painting depicts Cass Church, where thieves routinely steal our doorknobs and hardware.

Everything has been stolen from the church at least once. We've lost items you would expect, like hubcaps and car radios, purses, wallets, cash, credit cards, cameras, computers, candlesticks and microphones. Over time, we've had to add to the list anything "i"—iPads, iPods, iPhones …

But crooks have also taken things that you never would anticipate, like gutters and gates. One day, someone stole the historic marker from the front of the building. It wasn't made of scrap-worthy material. What do you do with a plaque that says "Cass Church was built in 1881"? Hang it on your house? Mount it on your boat? Attach it to your bike? Another thug came after that and left with a working toilet from the women's bathroom. Can you visualize being the next person to walk into the ladies' lavatory and finding a geyser where there used to be a ceramic toilet?

One night, a burglar rammed his pickup truck through the exterior kitchen wall and absconded with $700 worth of meat meant for the homeless. I ask you, how do you lock a wall? With apologies to my Universalist friends, I'd like to believe that there is a special circle in Dante's Inferno for folks who steal food intended for hungry people. Having said that, a community like Cass causes you to think deeply about crime and punishment. Everyone's extended family has someone who is incarcerated and everyone's extended family includes someone who has been the victim of a violent crime. Weekly prayer concerns include church members who are interceding for loved ones who are in jail, need a lawyer, have received a sentence, or are dealing with the consequences of a criminal record after being released from prison. One of my members will eventually be released from prison in a body bag. He received a life sentence at the age of 19 when he shot an ice cream delivery man to death.

Prayer requests from those who have been victims of crimes are likewise commonplace. I'll never forget the Sunday that Titus announced that he had been robbed. A quiet and hardworking teenager, Titus had grown up in Liberia, a country that was being torn apart by civil war. The children of Liberia were kept home from school because it was just too dangerous to be outside, even to walk through their own neighborhoods. When his mother died, Titus and his sister moved to Michigan to be raised by his uncle and aunt. He had to catch up with his peers academically, but it was apparent, within just a couple of months, that he was tenacious and focused. He was grateful for the opportunities in this country even if they had come as the result of his mother's death. Waiting for the bus in Detroit one morning, Titus was attacked by four gangsters, who held him up at gunpoint.

People rarely ask me my views on the criminal justice system. They aren't curious about what I believe in terms of policing, prosecuting, sentencing, incarcerating or paroling people. It's probably just as well because none of these topics are appropriate for sound bites. I could wax on for hours about what needs to be reformed.

Over the years, what people have asked me is if I'm scared to live or work in the city. I'm not and let me tell you why. Early on at Cass I recognized that many of the staff members were exhausted. People were working long, hard hours in stressful situations. So I told the employees of the Drop-In Center that they could have a day off with pay and that I would run the program in their absence.

The Drop-In Center was established in the late 1980s. Area shelters closed from 7 or 8 a.m. and didn't re-open until 6 or 7 p.m. Thus, the Cass Drop-In Center was created to provide those who were utilizing those shelters, and others—particularly people with mental illnesses who were living on the streets—with a safe haven where they could come to escape the elements and access basic services. Men, women and occasionally children came in to use the bathroom, talk on a telephone, get mail, wash their clothing, take a shower, use a computer, look for housing or a job. A couple of hundred people utilized the Cass program each day.

I arrived at 6 a.m. to open up. I started the coffee, turned on the electronic devices, and arranged the sign-up sheets for those wanting to take showers and do laundry. I noticed that there were piles of dirty towels and clothing as high as Mt. McKinley from the night before. I filled the washing machines with three loads of towels before I unlocked the doors. When the cycles stopped, I shifted the things to the dryers and began washing three more heaps. This went on all day long without interruption. In between cycles, I folded the items and managed to play a few games of chess with a couple of drop-in sharks.

At 6:00 p.m., one of the homeless volunteers announced that we would be closing soon. I looked around the laundry room for my jacket. It was gone. Actually, more important than my jacket, the keys to the kingdom were in my pocket— keys for the church, my car and my house. Not wanting to appear panicked, I mentioned the missing coat and keys to "Red," a tall, light-skinned African-American man who had actively given me unsolicited advice since the day I arrived. He turned and told the two people standing next to him, and they repeated it to those closest to them. Over and over, the message spread through the large room like a wildfire without a burn line. Within five minutes, 150 homeless men and women were scouring the streets to catch the villain who had appropriated my things. In fact, in record time, they found her and physically dragged her back into the building as if she was the woman caught in adultery. I was fearful that they were going to stone her right before my eyes. She stood frozen, except for one hand that thrust my coat and keys forward.

A look of panic crossed her face. Finally, in a voice that warbled uncontrollably, she uttered a tearful apology for all to hear. I told her to go and sin no more.

The episode taught me that the community has an intense empathy for those who have been wronged and that they would rise up to protect me if they could.

No, I'm not afraid at work.

Rotating Shelter

The Detroit-Wayne County Rotating Shelter was created to accommodate homeless people who couldn't get into the shelters in Detroit. There just weren't enough beds in the late 80s (and there still isn't an adequate number today). Here's how it works: Local churches agree to host "guests" who come from Cass during the evening hours, until the next morning, when our bus brings them back for the daytime. The rotating shelter churches supply dinner, a place to shower and sleep, breakfast and a sack lunch to get them through the next day.

It's an incredible program in so many ways. Churches of every size and stripe—Baptists, Catholics, Presbyterians, Lutherans, Methodists and non-denominational congregations—use their buildings, people and other resources for a week at a time to welcome strangers. The homeless guests experience the love of church volunteers—folks with both time and compassion. For their part, the church members begin to understand poverty, addiction, domestic violence and mental health issues as they spend time with the guests.

One drawback is that it is difficult to enlist enough congregations to fill the schedule from October through April. When there is a week that isn't covered by another church, the 50 to 80 homeless people stay at Cass Church. This sounds like a simple solution, but it is actually a taxing experience for everyone involved. All the other activities continue on as normal while we struggle to provide food and shelter for four or five extra weeks.

One of the most glaring mistakes I have made as a pastor came early on during one of our host weeks. It was Sunday morning and I announced that it was time for church. The men and women filed into the sanctuary, but it was apparent to everyone present that they didn't want to be there. They were digging through their garbage bags, talking, snoring, leaving to smoke or to use the bathroom or the phone. They certainly weren't doing the Methodist aerobics—nobody was standing at the right time, bowing their heads, pretending to sing, etc.

The services at Cass tend to last about an hour and a half most Sunday mornings and by the time we were done worshipping God I wanted to throttle them. I corralled all 80 people into the gym and rattled out a passionate tirade about showing respect to the congregation that makes sure that you have someplace to sleep and something to eat and somewhere to shower. "They give you shoes and coats and warm clothes and a place to do laundry … You will show them a measure of respect. Do you understand me?"

"Yes, Rev. Fowler … " they answered in unison.

"Good, because tonight you're going back to church," I said. You would have thought I said they were scheduled for circumcision procedures. Their faces became sad and sorry and solemn.

The evening service was even more casual and shorter in length. The guests proceeded into the sanctuary in single file and in utter silence, like a disciplined Marine unit. The men and women sang, stood, prayed and listened with uncommon attention. After the benediction, I congratulated myself on the lesson I had taught them.

Two weeks later, I would realize my mistake. The receptionist called me. "Rev. Fowler, Mr. Brown is here to see you." I didn't recognize the name but that was nothing new.

Frequently I would need to be reminded of who was who and how they were related to the ministry.

I went to the desk and spied a man I couldn't identify and beside him, a woman who was likewise a stranger to me. He extended his hand and acknowledged what must have been written all over my face, "You don't remember me, do you?"

"No," I confessed, "I'm sorry, I don't."

He replied, "I was in the Rotating Shelter when you made us go to church."

Oh my God, I thought to myself. He's got a lawyer. He's got a lawyer, he's going to sue us and he's going to win. You can't make anyone go to church. You can't make anyone sing religious songs. You can't make anyone pray or listen to a sermon. He's got a lawyer. He's going to sue us. He's going to win. My name is going to plastered on the front page of the Free Press and the News. The Bishop is going to appoint me to the moon. What am I going to do? "No," I said. "I don't remember you."

He replied, "I was in the Rotating Shelter when you *made* us go to church, and last week I got a job and I came to bring you my tithe."

In Cold Blood

I have stared into an oven as flames have consumed a casket and watched until the chamber door was opened so the remaining bone fragments and coffin nails could be swept out.

I have prayed with families who have struggled to reach the decision to withdraw life support and stood mute as ICU doctors weaned the family's loved one off mechanical ventilation.

I have held the trembling hands of a mother who could not believe that the car-struck body on the emergency room gurney was her lifeless 12-year-old son.

I have retrieved the noose from a garage before delivering a eulogy in a city church where the deceased's spouse didn't want others to know that the cause of death was suicide.

I have sobbed about the brevity of life and the emptiness of the universe before burying my father, my mother, two of my brothers, two uncles, two cousins and the children of two cousins.

But never have I experienced death's dagger the way that I did that morning when Bill stood up to speak. His emotion was raw. Unscripted, he said that his parents met at a private Michigan college and that they were both educated to serve as teachers. His father had been a music teacher and coached debate teams. His deceased mother was once an elementary school teacher in another suburban community.

Bill, the speaker in his early 60s, shared just enough stories from his childhood for the audience to know that he had been raised by good and loving parents. Then he told about their church and community involvements so we would understand that they had also been good people. In fact, a neighbor friend stopped by on the morning of September 7 to take Bill's dad, who was confined to a wheelchair, to their weekly Kiwanis meeting. The man knocked a couple of times and then let himself in through the unlocked front door. 87-year old Larry was lying on his side on the front room floor. The neighbor bent down and touched his shoulder when he noticed Larry's 85-year-old wife, Debra, likewise on the floor in a large pool of blood in the doorway to the kitchen. He called 911.

Larry had lost a lot of blood. He was confused, slipping in and out of consciousness. He had managed to hold on for 12 hours until the neighbor showed up. Debra was dead. When the first responders asked what happened, Larry replied, "Ronald." The paramedics added a question in route to Botsford Hospital. Who did this to you? Who beat you up? "Ronald did it," he answered again.

Bill paused before explaining that Ronald Edward Johnson had brutally attacked the couple. Bill's anger was no longer below the surface as he spoke. Listening to him was agonizing for me because they met Ronald when he was homeless and in the Cass Rotating Shelter program at their church in 1991. They befriended him, offered him work, bought him a used car, and invited him to spend the night at their home. Bill's parents were compassionate and generous Christians, but what did they get for all of their kindness?

Ronald robbed Larry and Debra in 1996. He took a car and money from their disabled daughter. Addicted to crack, he returned in 1998 and broke into their home to steal from them a second time, leaving the pair locked in their own basement when he left. Ronald was convicted of the crime and spent five years behind bars. Nevertheless, Debra understood his behavior as a cry for help and she was determined to do just that. She wrote him while he was incarcerated. She visited him, encouraged him and prayed with him. After he was paroled, she offered Ronald odd jobs once more and the couple received him as a regular overnight houseguest.

"I wish they had never met," Bill lamented. "He was a crazed drug addict. My mother let him into their home, and he struck her in the head and then beat her in the face after she fell to the ground. When my father called out from his bed to see what was happening, Ronald retrieved a knife from the kitchen and stabbed a defenseless man four times. He pulled my father's crippled body out of the bed and dropped him on the floor like a hundred pound barbell. Then, he returned to the bleeding heap that was my mother and viciously stabbed her.

"Listen to me. That animal should never have been allowed in the same room as my mother. He didn't deserve to breathe the same air. Maybe you think, like she did, that people can be redeemed, but Ronald didn't want to be saved. Drug addicts only care about getting drugs, getting high. Don't you let one more mugger into this church. Stop the program before someone else gets hurt."

He continued to talk and Debra's funeral lasted another 40 minutes or so, but my mind stopped functioning.

Larry remained in a coma for 16 more days.

By the time he died, Ronald had been apprehended. After two bad tips, the police received a call from Crime Stoppers that led them right to Ronald. He was sitting on a park bench at Gratiot and St. Aubin. He had gone into the 7th Precinct the day before to turn himself in for the homicide, but the officer at the desk told him to get the "f--k" out of the police station.

Ronald was cooperative with the arresting officers. The police transported him back to the 7th Precinct. There he was booked, fingerprinted, photographed and interviewed after he waived his Miranda rights. Ronald explained that he had gotten off work, driven to Detroit to get high and then gone to the couple's house about 9:30 p.m. Debra let him in even though she was on the phone with one of her sons. When she hung up, she talked with Ronald for about 10 minutes. She walked out of the room; he followed her. He struck her in the head. She fell down immediately.

Ronald claimed that he didn't know why he'd done what he had. The detective asked if he had gone there to rob the couple. No, Ronald responded. He didn't need money. He had money in his pockets. Pressed by the officer, Ronald said that he didn't understand why he killed them. He reflected that Debra was the only person he'd ever really loved; she'd been like a mother.

The officer told Ronald that it would be great if we could turn back time and change everything that occurred, but that we can't. We have to face what has happened—and so do all the people who have been forced to cope with the wreckage.

Lottery Losers

Not every homeless person is a murderer. In fact, homeless folks are much more likely to be victims of violence than to be perpetrators of it. Nor is every homeless individual a drug addict or an alcoholic. It is true that many struggle to obtain and maintain sobriety, but so do many in society as a whole.

People become homeless for a variety of reasons, including addiction, mental illness, physical illness, domestic violence, discrimination due to sexual preference or gender identity, the loss of a job or the death of a family member. Large numbers of men and women returning from war or coming out of prison end up homeless too, because the transition can be as challenging as climbing Mt. Everest. Some people experience a combination of these causes.

Then, there are other homeless people who tend to be lazy and rebellious. It's as if they are allergic to work. They don't want others telling them what to do. They revolt against discipline or authority. These people are homeless because they are children who didn't win the parent lottery. This is not to say that they have horrible parents, but that their fate was determined by having a homeless parent or parents.

In 1998, the city asked Cass to open a nightly Warming Center for homeless women and children. Immediately, people began arriving with stories instead of luggage. After two months of couch surfing, one woman's welcome had run out. Her friends dropped her and her young family off at Cass Church like dirty laundry is left on the counter of a dry cleaner. Another woman and her three children had lived in their car on Belle Isle, a city park, for several weeks. The kids cleaned up in the public restrooms before she took them to their respective schools each morning. She did day labor when she could find it. At night, they ran the car engine long enough to take the chill out of the air. As the fall temperatures dropped, running the motor became too expensive and they came inside.

One woman walked in. She had given birth to a baby boy four days prior and had hiked the eight blocks from Receiving Hospital after being discharged. Her newborn wasn't strapped into a car seat or a pastel-colored stroller. The baby was in a tattered cardboard box, about the size of a banker's box but minus the handles and lined with a donated blue baby blanket. I dipped my head down to smell the child's new-to-the-world skin sprinkled with baby powder. He was so tiny and vulnerable, totally dependent on a woman who had neither a roof nor a refrigerator.

Most parents dream about what their child will become—a doctor, a dancer, a lawyer, an actor, a business leader or even the president. It is almost as if once a baby begins to breathe independently, there is a second pregnancy—one of expectations. That's what made the predicament so tragically sad. The lines etched on the woman's face made it clear that she wasn't dreaming of future possibilities as she rocked the child in her arms. She was dreading what might happen to him. She knew first-hand that the odds of escaping crushing poverty are akin to those of winning a Nobel Prize. Although anything is possible, statistically, her little boy didn't have a prayer.

Caroline

You could earn a Purple Heart at Cass just for taking the trash out. I am always afraid that an animal is going to attack me, like the gopher in Caddyshack. Scavenger mice, possums, raccoons, rats and stray cats frequently shoot out of the dumpsters when you lift a lid or open one of the green sliding doors. Still, I had no idea that a person could scare me the way Caroline did.

She was buried in the waste, sandwiched between black garbage bags. Lost in her own tortured world, she vaulted up, muttering something that I couldn't decipher. She smelled like the sewer, her black winter coat was covered in rot and garbage.

"Are you OK?" I managed to ask despite the overpowering rush of adrenalin.

Again, she made noises more than words. Caroline appeared irritated that I had disrupted her.

"Why don't you come inside? I'll get you something to eat." I was guessing that she had crawled into the steel Waste Management container to scoop up the scraps of food mixed in with the rubbish. She probably just fell asleep inside. It happens sometimes. I know a man who did and woke up only when he heard the trash compactor start up. He screamed for his life.

Caroline started shouting and waving her arms wildly, as a way to push me away. Her voice grew louder and louder until I vanished into the church. I loaded up a plate with a slab of meatloaf, some mashed potatoes and green peas. Then I grabbed a napkin and silverware before returning to the dark alleyway. She started yelling again. I placed the dinner on the concrete stairs and walked away. From the other end of the block, I could see that she was eating the dinner with her hands.

For the next month, the kitchen crew made Caroline three meals a day and left all of them on the kitchen steps. Sometimes staff members watched through a crack in the door, but they always left her alone. Then one day, Caroline astonished us all when she came in. She sat in a corner of the gym, isolating herself in a room crammed full of people. It would require several more weeks before she joined the Rotating Shelter.

During the daytime hours, when the rotating guests were at Cass, Pat Green, the homeless services director at that time, would make announcements as if they were for general consumption:

"If there is anyone here named Caroline, who would like to go into a special program that we're going to offer this summer, come and see me." The staff members were clueless about Pat's strategy. Still, it worked. Caroline approached Pat one day. The shelter was about to close down for the summer and Pat told her that Cass had a safe place just for her to go as long as she was willing to work with the case manager there. Caroline consented.

We moved her to Mom's Place, since it was the only program we had for women at the time. The program was designated for homeless women and their children. Caroline slept on a sofa and Pat continued putting ideas in the universe. One day, she told Caroline that if she would consent to spend some time in the hospital, Cass would have a job for her when she came out. These conversations about treatment and employment were repeated over and over, every day for weeks. Finally,

Caroline agreed to get help. We took her in to the crisis center, but after the van pulled away, Caroline exited herself. Like a boomerang, she came back to Cass. She nearly beat the driver back to the church.

Next, Pat began saying that it would be easier for Caroline if she allowed us to commit her to the hospital. This is the purgatory of mental health treatment today. Large numbers of individuals with mental health issues are convinced that they do not need help and unless they are violent, suicidal or homicidal, it is nearly impossible to assist them. Minus mental health services, including medications, most are unable to lead happy or productive lives. So again, Pat Green started endless discussions with Caroline. Fortunately, Caroline was ultimately persuaded. Our staff drove her back to the crisis center once more. This time she was admitted and stayed for 10 days.

When she returned to Cass, Caroline's enthusiasm couldn't be contained. Physically, she appeared changed—rested and happy. Caroline's clothes were clean and pressed and colorful. She wore a trace of make-up and a lightly scented perfume. What's more, she was able to articulate her story to us for the first time. She had been evicted from her house and was forced to stay in an emergency shelter with her daughter. One night there she had a grand mal seizure and ended up in the emergency room. Her older sister came and took both Caroline's daughter and her car.

When she was discharged from the hospital, Caroline returned to the homeless shelter and learned that she couldn't get back into the emergency program due to her previous health scare. She walked to another shelter, which didn't have any open beds. Then she began calling agencies, none of them had available space. Caroline had a psychotic breakdown because she couldn't find housing—and couldn't get her daughter back without it. She took to sleeping in the parks, at bus stops and in alleys. An alley, of course, is where I found her dressed in black, goth-style like a teenager and covered in rancid waste and flies.

Pat Green was true to her word. Cass created a job and hired Caroline to work part-time in the clothing closet. When Mom's Place II opened for single women, we were able to move Caroline there. Within 18 months, the woman we had once called "Legion," had furniture, an apartment, a full-time job, and, after winning in court, was reunited with her daughter. Not every story ends this way, but in this one they lived happily ever after.

NIMBY

One unusual thing about my house is that it shares a backyard with the duplex next door. On the one hand, this is a
fabulous reality in that the area is private, surrounded on the
exterior by an eight foot panel fence, and pastoral with trees
and grass and gardens that you'd never expect in the middle of an urban area. There are birds, bats, squirrels, possums,
and, occasionally, rats for the dogs to chase. One of the former
duplex residents actually owned a flying dog named Zimba,
which she smuggled out of Africa after she finished her term
with the Peace Corps. Standing still, Zimba could levitate
straight up in the air to catch birds in mid-flight.

The less fortunate fact about the common backyard was the
in-ground pool. I know what you are thinking. How could
there be a problem with a pool? The neighbors maintained
it, so the chlorinated water was always crystal clear and, with
the tall fence, someone drowning wasn't really a concern. No,
the issue with the pool was that sometimes the neighbors
and their friends swam naked. Perhaps you are an exhibition-
ist and you don't mind seeing or showing private parts. Or,
maybe you are just a voyeur … Not me. Keep your outfits on.
Swim in a bathing suit is my mantra. There are very few people who look attractive minus coverings. So, for the first time
in my life, I joined the NIMBY chorus, "Not in My Backyard."

In reality, there are plenty of things I'd prefer to keep out of my backyard—like the residents of the zoo's reptile house or an angry armed militia or unsupervised birthday parties for children under seven. There are things I like to avoid in my front yard, too, like hundreds of sticky plastic beer cups left over from the St. Patrick's Day Parade or fresh rank piles of poop from someone else's dog. These things I don't even want in my alley. You can count on me to join all of these NIMBY groups.

The difficulty is that the undesirable things most NIMBY people organize against are things that we need, services that most people want provided—just in someone else's space. Things like prisons, halfway houses, rehab facilities, methadone clinics, adult foster care homes, and low-income housing. NIMBY objectors tend to acknowledge the need to reduce crime, encourage sobriety and get people into housing, but they stand vehemently and vocally firm that the services must be delivered elsewhere.

Thus, there are scores of NIMBY activities which end up in the same somebody else's backyard. In fact, when I arrived at Cass Church, the local leaders wasted no time in telling me that the area was saturated with social services and that there was a moratorium on any new programs. They were not cold or callous people. Rather, they were convinced that the shelters and soup kitchens were acting as a huge magnet, drawing every homeless, alcoholic, mentally ill or poor person from all five metropolitan counties into the Cass Corridor.

I was ambivalent about how to be a good neighbor and, at the same time, how to provide more than just emergency services. In 1995, Cass secured a Housing and Urban Development (HUD) grant to establish Michigan's first Safe Haven for homeless men with severe mental illnesses. We had planned to renovate the Marie apartment building next to the church for the residential program. After sinking $150,000 into pre-development fees, though, we discovered that the Marie was structurally unsound due to a few arson fires, so, the cost per unit for the rehab was prohibitive. The decision to look outside the area was made for me.

Mike Hickey, a Detroit real estate agent, started searching for properties that could accommodate the 21-person program. He provided leads and we took small teams of staff members to survey the spaces and the surroundings. Each resident would need a room. The staff would require offices and areas for medication storage, group sessions and food preparation. The building needed to be close to public transportation as well as basic shopping. Moreover, I had an antenna up for drug and other criminal activities that might tempt our men to engage in risky behaviors. It was slim pickings once all of the criteria were considered.

Mike was able to identify a mid-sized brick building with apartments above some commercial space on a main artery of the city. The square footage was adequate, the price was reasonable and the repairs required were minimal. We were ecstatic. Then, Mike called to say that members of the area community association wanted to meet with us. Mind you, we hadn't even submitted a bid on the property yet.

At the meeting, our homeless director offered a succinct history of Cass and explained the Safe Haven philosophy before opening the floor up for comments and questions. As you might expect, the members of the association asked about safety and security. Yes, the property would be staffed around the clock. Then, someone mentioned that there had been a rape recently a few blocks away.

I took a turn, selecting my words as cautiously as a soldier steps to avoid hidden land mines.

"Mental illness is a disease, a brain disease, but a disease nonetheless. People with mental illnesses are not different from people with physical diseases like cancer or diabetes," I said, hoping to change the collective hearts of those in the room.

"They need to take medicine, just as someone uses antibiotics or, better yet, insulin that must be taken every day. With the right kind of medicine and the right drug dosage, people with bipolar disorder or schizophrenia or depression can be good tenants and citizens. The residents will be supported and supervised in a way that whoever committed the recent rape probably wasn't. I can't guarantee you that these men will never get in trouble, but I can promise you that the Safe Haven staff will monitor them closely and that we will be involved in this community so you will know them and they will know you.

"We are committed to being good neighbors," I remained calm while speaking. "The Cass staff and residents will help with clean-up days, and they will volunteer with the neighborhood radio patrol. If you know of a senior or a handicapped individual who can't maintain their grass or shovel their snow, we will help. The staff will be attentive to our building and they will make sure that no one is loitering out front ... "

They weren't having any of it. "NOT IN MY BACKYARD!" one leader exploded, adding a line quoted by every upset NIMBY person I had ever met. "Why don't you establish the program where you live?"

Just as someone with multiple personalities slips into another identity to avoid trauma, I responded to his rant by thinking about how funny his suggestion was, given where I live. My house sits on the western edge of Corktown, in the shadows of the deserted Michigan Central Depot and the old Roosevelt Hotel. The latter was converted into a homeless shelter before a fire shut down the facility. After the shelter closed, homeless people and squatters regularly moved in and out. Frequently, as if watching television, the temporary residents stared down at my neighbors in the pool. There weren't any window treatments, or even window panes in the former shelter to obstruct their view.

"Here's the thing," I said, though I could read the writing on the wall. "We are only talking about 21 men in a small apartment building." The crowd was glassy-eyed. With the timing of synchronized swimmers, they folded their arms across their chests to nonverbally communicate their unanimous rejection.

Maybe the only fair way to do the things that we agree are needed is to establish a rotation, so that every neighborhood or ZIP code area periodically has a program for "undesirable" activities. One year your backyard would have a small prison (it doesn't seem fair that the rural areas have most of the prisons or that a large percentage of prisoner families have to travel great distances to visit their relatives). The next year, you get an AFC home. A year after that, you win a homeless shelter. We could put almost everything on stilts and wheels to make the swap easier. Naturally, if your neck of the woods had the stationary nuclear power plant, you'd pretty much be stuck with it, but your neighborhood would never have to tolerate more than that undesirable.

Opposition to the Safe Haven was everywhere. The process cost us precious time and money. Never mind that most people continued to believe that warehousing folks for years in state hospitals is fundamentally wrong or that most also recognize the tragic "frequent flier" patterns of mentally ill people in emergency rooms and prisons.

Mike finally found a building just three miles north of the Cass Church building, directly off the Lodge Freeway. It was the old ob-gyn annex of the former Florence Crittenton Hospital. The place was vacant, but it was a solid structure. He contacted the owners and met up with their representatives in the parking lot next to the 30,000 square foot building. When they learned that he was interested in buying the property, one of the people nearly ran Mike over with his pickup truck. We were off to a good start.

Tenacious, Mike wouldn't take no for an answer. Two meetings later, I got my first look inside. I walked through the vacant structure enamored. The patient examining rooms were the perfect size for bedrooms. Each floor had a lounge with plenty of natural light where residents could gather for group time or to meet visitors. The first floor included a file room that we could convert into educational space for GED classes, computer classes, literacy classes and financial management classes. It had an entire wing for administrative staff offices, and the basement could be developed in the future for a commercial kitchen, pantry, lunchroom and laundry room.

When the owners read newspaper articles about million dollar HUD awards slated for Michigan, they increased the building's purchase price twice. Renovating the facility required two more years after the closing. By then, we had secured a second HUD grant to provide transitional housing for 21 homeless men with chronic substance abuse. There was ample room for both residential programs and the property included about six acres of land, so there was even room to expand. We built a garden-like courtyard so the residents could enjoy the outdoors and no one would complain about people loitering.

Today, the residents from both floors regularly volunteer to help with neighborhood clean-up days when we eliminate blight, and board-up days when vacant structures are secured.

By the way, now that we are located in somebody's backyard, the local community association meets in our building every month.

CHAPTER 4

Housing

There's Something About That Name

On the day after Thanksgiving, I took a change-your-life kind of trip. I went to the Humane Society to pick out a dog. Dogs are evidence that unconditional love exists. A few friends and I walked from cage to cage, looking for the perfect animal. I really wanted a Lab but decided against it because the breed tends to be too heavy to carry. Finally, I zeroed in on a year-old chow, shepherd and pit bull mix. He weighed about 40 pounds and sported a thick, handsome burnt red and blonde coat.

A paper sign on the dog's cage explained that Dale, the husband of one of the kennel staff members, had found the dog wandering outside. Dale brought the pup into the Chrysler Drive location—instead of bringing his wife lunch—and the canine was immediately seen by Dr. Smaller due to a gash in his paw. The notice also indicated that the wound had been covered by a homemade bandage and that coins were attached to the dog's collar in place of a name tag.

That's the thing about stray dogs—you usually don't know their names. It was true for this mid-sized mongrel. So the Humane Society staff gave him the less than flattering new name: Jughead. Perhaps they had witnessed his reaction to thunderstorms—one of his bouts of heavy panting, constant pacing and destroying anything in his path. Or maybe they had heard him loudly barking at a bicycle, a motorcycle, a truck, a squirrel or the vacuum. Whatever caused them to name him after a cartoon character, he would need another new name if he was going to live with me. I decided to call him Tank, because he was built like one.

After he was sterilized, I took Tank home. Actually, he went with me to work, as he would almost every day. Some people have suggested over the years that the practice was good for my safety, but it had nothing to do with that. All anyone would have to do to get around my "security dog" would be to offer him a hot dog or ice cream or Chinese food. Tank has a fondness for the last two food types thanks to Maximo Ki Ki Jorrin, a Cuban man who started in our residential programs and now works as part of the Cass staff.

Ki Ki feeds, walks and occasionally sleeps with Tank. No, I have hauled Tank into work every day because he makes the homeless shelter more humane and because I would never forgive myself if someone broke into my house and hurt my adopted dog.

Tank's middle name is Lucifer. I'm sure you can guess why. He has been possessed since that first day at the church. Tank would infuriate the finance director by nipping at his butt as Bob stood duplicating reports at the copy machine. Tank developed a reputation for intimidating folks who were afraid of him—barking, jumping, chasing them down the hall or out of the office. Never mind that you couldn't leave any food unattended on the table. Even eating your own lunch in his presence was a trick. When he wasn't terrorizing or begging, Tank sat in my office window sill as if he were a cat. One day, he proved his above average intelligence by pulling down the handicap-friendly door lever to let himself out of a locked office. Tank Lucifer is his name. It signifies that just as he is built like a truck, he is full of the devil.

All this is to say that names should mean something. Biblical names usually do. Moses, who was tucked into a basket as a baby and released on the Nile, means "to draw out." Cain, who murdered his brother Abel, means "spear." David, who was anointed while Saul was still king, means "hero." Bathsheba and Uriah may have objected to the designation, but that is another story. In both Hebrew Scripture and Christian texts, naming involved a process and it defined a person's nature. A name told not only who a person was, but what. Consequently, biblical parents didn't just select something casually from a book of names. They didn't make up some hard to pronounce, nonsensical name either. They selected mostly hard to pronounce names that meant something.

When a name is changed in Scripture, it signifies that there had been a shift in identity. Advanced in age, Abram became Abraham and Sari changed to Sarah because they would become parents to many nations. Saul was switched to Paul, following his conversion on the road to Damascus. The stories suggest a person does not have a name. You are a name but, unlike the animals named by Adam, both you and your name can change. A new name marks transformation.

We have tried to select meaningful names for each of the Cass Community Social Services buildings. Our first facility was originally the ob-gyn annex for Crittenton Hospital. While the building was under construction, Charlotte Scott, our receptionist, was killed by a man she had known since high school but with whom she became reacquainted one day at Cass Church. The two had an argument at her home. The man struck her with a piece of wood. As she lay bleeding, he helped himself to some of her belongings, including her car, but he never called for help. Charlotte died and the man went to prison for the crime. We renamed the old hospital building in memory of Charlotte Scott.

Someone once asked why we would dedicate a building for Charlotte when we could have used the naming opportunity to raise a lot of money. The answer is simple. Charlotte's premature and violent death affected everyone at Cass. She was just 28, gregarious and vibrant. While performing her duties at the receptionist's desk, she greeted each person who came in the door or called on the phone. When she wasn't engaged in conversation, Charlotte was snacking, making up lyrics to songs or laughing too loud. Members of the staff cared about her. They attended her funeral and, the next day, they all returned to work. So it was that our name selection honored Charlotte's short life, but also all of the other Cass employees who understood that there are risks involved in trying to help others.

The next residential program that required a building ended up in a rented storefront church because we were only given two weeks to have the program operational. Since the facility didn't belong to us, we named the transitional housing program Mom's Place instead. When two generous and anonymous donors made it possible to relocate the program onto the Cass campus in 2008, naming became an issue once more. The purchased buildings were unnamed but both belonged to the former Lula Belle Stewart organization. Lula Belle Stewart was an African-American doctor who practiced at Crittenton Hospital. Since we weren't providing medical services in the buildings, we re-named them using the program name, Mom's Place I and II.

In 2005, Cass was awarded one of eight HOPWA grants in the country to establish permanent supportive housing for homeless men living with HIV/AIDS. Just seven years after the heinous homophobic attack on Matthew Shepard and a little less than a year after Daniel Fetty, a gay hearing-impaired homeless man who suffered an equally ruthless and senseless assault in Waverly, Ohio, we knew that for all the red ribbons, our building would need to be nondescript in every way. Never do we disclose its address, show pictures of the property or publish the program's telephone number. We inherited the building thanks to the work of Linda MacQueen and it is our nicest facility inside and out—but it is never included on our tours. We simply call it Cass House. When the hate crimes stop and the fear dissipates, we will gladly rename the building.

We absorbed a Roman Catholic nonprofit organization called Oasis Detroit in 2011. Their staff had been doing extraordinary work with formerly homeless men and women with mental illnesses. An Irish Franciscan with a passion for this population, Father Mel Brady was one of the founding board members. When we moved Oasis Detroit onto the Cass campus, it made perfect sense to name the program's facility after the late priest, so it became the Brady Building.

Then Cass took over a program for formerly homeless women and children with HIV/AIDS, which had been operated by Simon House. We renamed the apartment building for a Cass Church board member, Helen Bernauer. By the time I met Helen in 1994, she was using a walker to get around, but she was still certainly a dynamo. Helen had helped organize everything in the church and most of the community organizations, including the 4 C's (Concerned Citizens of the Cass Corridor), CCYA (Cass Corridor Youth Advocates), CCNDC (Cass Corridor Neighborhood Development Corporation) and CCSS (Cass Community Social Services). Everything that ever amounted to anything was first discussed at her dining room table—a table known to tempt you with candies strategically placed in the center, surrounded year-round by Christmas decorations, tree included. Her name is forever linked with the other board members who joined her at the table like Ray and Louise Travis, Irene Giles, Carol Shissler, Lillis Cunningham, Cassie Hornady, Louise Abernathy, Ann Scott …

Finally, our most ambitious housing facility was named for Arthur Antisdel, a CCSS board member and a distinguished Wayne State University professor of social work. He was a champion of several causes: labor and unions, high school drop-outs, infant mortality. Art volunteered his time and expertise to Cass before, during and after the nonprofit was established. He served on CCSS's Board of Directors until his death in 2003.

Soon after I arrived at Cass, people were talking about re-branding the area—changing the name of the neighborhood from the Cass Corridor to Midtown. The area was originally part of the Cass farm. Lewis Cass was the territorial governor from 1813 until 1831. In 1836, he became the Secretary of War under Andrew Jackson. He served as the American ambassador to France and as a U.S. Senator from 1845 until 1857, with the exception of the year he ran for president. The corridor designation referred to the fact that the area was bounded by freeways or major roads.

I'm still not sure what Midtown means. We're certainly not midway between downtown and 8 Mile. Maybe the name connotes that the area if halfway between the Detroit River and New Center. Clearly, we're not a town at all. What is true is that the neighborhood has changed dramatically. Some refer to it as gentrification. There is new housing stock, businesses and restaurants. This has improved the city's tax base and added numerous quality of life options in the area. These changes have come with a price tag though. Long-time residents and poor people are divided about the tradeoffs.

Superman

The Ambassadors Gospel Choir was organized almost immediately after we opened the Scott Building. You just had to hear someone singing in the hallway to know that the building was bursting with untapped talent.

I called Gladys Ferguson, the volunteer coordinator, into my office and explained to her that I wanted a choir. Gladys is a 5-foot-4-inch slender African-American woman who tends to be clad in an oversized sweatshirt, fake black leather pants and flat-soled shoes. The exception is when she is directing the choir. For performances, she adds a glitter jacket over the sweatshirt and slacks and dons a Whoopi Goldberg wig right out of *Sister Act*. Her wig collection includes eight or 10 styles. It is rare to see her without one. I'll never forget the day when I was with her standing in line for a roller coaster at Cedar Point. That's when Gladys whipped off her wig and tied it to the belt loop of her blue jeans so she wouldn't lose it on the ride.

Gladys exited the nearest door and bellowed, "Can anybody sing?" And the rest, as they say, is history. From the very beginning, about a dozen men volunteered their time and extraordinary talent. Over the years, the composition of the group has changed as men have come and gone from the residential programs, but the number has remained constant, as has the quality of their vocal gifts. Only a couple of choir members have had limited talent.

Probably the least endowed was Albert.

He looked like one of the disciples from da Vinci's Last Supper. He had long, stringy, dirty blonde hair. His beard was unkempt and he was as skinny as a rail. When he arrived at Cass, he seldom spoke, and if he did, he had a flat affect. So it surprised Gladys when one day, he approached her and asked if he could join the choir.

Gladys took him in without an audition. He stood out immediately because just as he didn't talk, Albert didn't sing. He just stood there and swayed slightly, mostly counter to the rest of the group. Being white, he fit the stereotype—Albert had no rhythm at all. Our politically incorrect joke was that if we could get Albert to clap on time and the rest of the group to arrive on time … you get the gist of it.

Still, he was faithful. He was a fixture at the rehearsals in the classroom. He traveled with the men when they went on the road to perform at various church and community engagements.

Once, the group traveled up north to sing for a bunch of youth who were going to sleep outside for the night in cardboard boxes to experience "homelessness." The Ambassadors belted out five or six songs before Gladys asked if any of them would share their testimonies.

Miracle of miracles, Albert volunteered.

He told the teens that he had been staying with his sister, living on a cot in the basement of her house. Evidently the space was dark and damp and dirty. He shared the lower level with an assortment of rodents. Albert commented that his sister was oblivious to his situation because she was busy using and selling narcotics. It was there that he started using heroin. One night, the house was raided by Detroit police. Albert was comatose in his bed and only remembered what others told him about the foray. He woke up at the hospital. He was so completely out of it, he said, that the doctors had toe tagged him.

Most of the time on an Ambassadors road trip, I would fulfill two special roles. I served as the designated driver and as their warm-up act. It was my job to get the crowd to settle down and be receptive to the group. Many times, the Ambassadors seemed strange to the crowds. The church people we would perform for often don't know any homeless people, people of color, men who had served time, adults with mental illnesses, or folks who have struggled with addiction to alcohol and illegal drugs. We are all of those.

I talk first in an effort to break the ice. Generally, I use humor. Once at a church in Garden City, I re-told a slightly modified rendition of a story I had read by Charlene Ann Baumbich. It involves a couple who are having a conversation when the husband starts to sneeze.

The man, I tell the crowd, is honking like Felix from *The Odd Couple*—loud and wet and disgusting. But since they have been together so long, she keeps talking. The husband then reaches into his pocket and retrieves a handkerchief. I always add that he has to be at least middle-aged because young men don't know what a handkerchief is.

The wife watches her husband but continues speaking while he clears his nasal cavities. After her husband finishes honking and wiping his nose, he folds the handkerchief exactly on the creases and places it back in his back pocket.

Her jaw drops to the ground.

Her mate says, "Is something wrong?"

She replies, "Do you always do that?"

"Do what?" he's befuddled.

"After you finish blowing your nose, do you always fold up your handkerchief and put it back into your pocket?" she asks.

"Yes," he answers, "is that a problem?"

"I would say it is. For 25 years, whenever I do the laundry and come across a handkerchief in your pants pocket, I have assumed that you didn't use it so I put it back in your drawer."

The crowd always becomes hysterical at this point until I interrupt them with the conclusion of the story.

Then his jaw drops.

"Is something wrong?" she asks.

"Yes," he answers.

"What's wrong?" she asks.

"Well, I guess that explains why for 25 years I haven't been able to get my glasses clean."

The church hoots and chuckles like children. No one remains nervous. The Ambassadors blow them away with their gospel songs. The group mingles with the church members for way too many snacks and beverages in the fellowship hall. The kitchen crew loads our van up with goodies to take back. Over and out.

I don't think a thing about the average concert after that. But one night I was standing at the van waiting for the group to come out and load up for a performance. Albert emerged alone and said to me, "I'm ready."

"Good," I responded, wondering what is taking everyone else so long. I hate to arrive late.

"Rev. Fowler, I'm ready."

"Great."

A third time, he repeated, "I'm ready."

"What are you ready for?" I asked.

To which Albert responded, "I've got my glasses and a handkerchief in case you want to tell that story again."

This was my Clark Kent moment at Cass. You remember Clark—he was a reporter, sort of a geeky guy, with way too much hair product and a pocket protector and a girlfriend named Lois Lane ...

Somehow he was always in tune with crime and bad things. He would disappear into a telephone booth, spin around rapidly like a particularly buff Olympic figure skater, so that his features became a blur behind the glass panels. When he emerged, he was a superhero in a red and blue costume that included tights and a cape. As Superman, he would launch into the air and fly "faster than a locomotive, able to leap tall buildings in a single bound." What's more, he righted things.

And the point to all this—Clark Kent and Superman were the same person even if no one recognized it. They had identical eyes, the same voice, and matching fingerprints, yet they were entirely different.

Albert had been declared dead. He has a toe tag to prove it. But there he was standing in our parking lot telling me that he had heard my borrowed story and that he wanted to help reenact it. He wanted to belong and participate. He was resurrected like Lazarus. He never did learn to clap on time, but nobody cares.

God's Country

The Ambassadors Choir adopted a grueling schedule in its first year and a half. The men performed for the Elks, Lions and the Kiwanis. They entertained church folks for Advent and Lent. Some weeks they were on the road three or four nights, and so we decided to reward them with a tour. We lined up several stops in Michigan's Upper Peninsula, God's Country, for a week in September when the fall colors would be at their peak.

It was August when I realized that the formerly homeless men didn't have the things required for a getaway. They lacked luggage and swimsuits. (And who wants to spend the night in a hotel without swimming in the pool or sitting in the Jacuzzi?)

Now you are going to know that I own a dog and have never raised children. I went to Meijer, a great Michigan retail company, to purchase the needed items. Suitcases weren't a problem, but the swimsuits were another matter altogether. Mothers know that you can't buy a swimsuit in Michigan in August. So I decided to pick up some basketball shorts. They are long and fit a variety of body types, thanks to the drawstring. I picked out University of Michigan colors, maize and blue.

We drove straight up the I-75 expressway to the Mackinac Bridge. Crossing over the bridge, I fished for a compliment: "Anybody ever been to the U.P. before?" I was expecting to hear back: No, Rev. Fowler—this is great! Thanks so much for bringing us! It feels so good to spend time outside the city!

What I heard was, "Yeah, but the last time I was in shackles."

Evidently at that time Victor had been the youngest prisoner, just a teenager, sentenced to serve time in Marquette. He talked about how scared he had been and the fact that no one from his family came to see him due to the prison's distance from Detroit. (It is a shorter distance to travel to Washington, D.C. than it is to travel from Detroit to parts of the Upper Peninsula.)

This time, the trip was different. There were jokes and songs and the recognition of beauty as the passenger van rolled along the two-lane highway that hugged Lake Michigan.

That night, the men performed at a mid-sized church in Escanaba. About 150 people were there to hear them sing and listen to their personal stories. But something was wrong. It was funeral home quiet. No one clapped. No one moved. I thought to myself: *We're in trouble. We better get out of here quick as soon as the choir is done.*

There was polite applause at the concert's conclusion. The pastor announced refreshments in the narthex and then, I noticed that a woman from the audience approached an Ambassador as he stood on the chancel platform. She handed him her program and a pen and asked him if he would sign it. In the blink of an eye, others formed more than one queue in front of the men as if they were waiting on the red carpet outside the Oscars for autographs. From that point on, the Ambassadors expected paparazzi to greet them in each new city.

When we returned to the hotel that night, the men headed down to the pool, and I followed closely behind them. The hotel receptionist stopped me. "Is that the University of

Michigan basketball team?" he asked. "Yes," I lied. We had great service there.

The following day, we traveled even further northwest to Houghton. The small town is home to Michigan Tech and its Winter Carnival. We were welcomed there at the Methodist Church by an illuminated lawn sign that announced the Ambassadors' concert. Once more, the group sang inspiring spirituals, and individuals spoke about their episodes of homelessness and their plans for the future.

Steve shared that his experience was tied to addiction and he talked about the impact that his drug use had on his parents. His speech had a profound impact on a woman in the crowd. She approached him on the sidewalk outside afterward. She wanted Steve to know that in listening to his story, she was able to come to terms with her daughter's drug dependence. For the first time, the mother said while sobbing, she realized that it was not her fault.

Addiction, just as it cuts across class, race, gender and age brackets, is no respecter of peninsulas. It is everywhere unfortunately, so the need for understanding and recovery and healing is everywhere, too. Steve's willingness to be vulnerable that night set at least one family free.

Fourth Time's The Charm

The Salvation Army called on a Wednesday afternoon in 2008. I remember distinctly because the caller told me that a local women's shelter had to be closed immediately. Could we accommodate 50 women and children by Friday? "Sure," I answered, though I wasn't sure at all. What else could I say? The number of homeless mothers and children had been skyrocketing since the elimination of General Assistance in Michigan.

Our 54-passenger bus made two trips to the closing shelter. The first run was for the people standing out in front of the vacant building; the second was to retrieve their clothing and other belongings. The possessions were stacked up in plastic trash bags as if waiting for collection by a garbage truck. The people and their property met up at a laundromat prior to reaching their final destination. Our policy is to launder everything before someone moves in to minimize the possibility that they will be bringing along bed bugs or lice.

Lice are relatively easy to eradicate. Using medicated shampoo will take care of head lice, body lice or pubic lice after a shower or two as long as you wash and dry the person's clothing and bedding at the same time. Bed bugs are another story. Once an area is infested with these blood-sucking parasites, it takes an all-out effort and a huge war chest to eliminate them.

Call in the reinforcements. The male bed bugs are sex crazed. Often, they pierce the females' abdomens rather than wasting time with their reproductive tracts. No Luther Vandross. No romantic candles. No flowers or dinner. No. It's wham, bam, thank you ma'am. Then, the female bed bugs wander all over the place, laying their eggs randomly on clothing and bedding but also in bed frames and mattresses, shoes, slippers, furniture, books, bags and electronics. Those little mothers lay eggs on the walls and in electric outlets. Fertilized females can lay three or four eggs a day for months. They don't even have to eat every day to stay healthy.

So, you are forced to call a professional exterminator. (Do-it-yourself sprays don't worry bed bugs.) Before the pest control company arrives, people have to move all the furniture away from the walls. They have to take down all the molding and remove the outlet plates. They must open and empty their cabinets and drawers. Residents need to bag up all of their clothing—clean and dirty—so they can wash and dry it while the premises are being steam-cleaned or treated chemically. Miss one bag, one drawer, one room, and you have to repeat the entire process. You can't just take a mattress outside either, because then you are scattering the pests, rather than killing them. The cost for bed bug control at Cass is as much as $30,000 to $40,000 annually, even with our precautions.

With 50 people coming at once, we were going to make sure no one was bringing bugs into our building. Although you can apply 99 percent alcohol using a spray bottle to kill bed bugs, it doesn't work with eggs. Instead, the women were taken to the laundromat to clean and dry all of their things. It was there that one woman shared with me that her family had been homeless four times. Her name was Stephanie.

Stephanie was one of the thousands who didn't have the means to escape Hurricane Katrina. Her loved ones stuffed themselves into the attic of their New Orleans home. They were safe and dry, but stranded. When it became clear that help wasn't on the way, her husband managed to smash a hole in the roof using only a flashlight. A very pregnant Stephanie, her husband and their toddler waded in contaminated water to get to the Superdome, where they spent six terrifying days. She talked about weeping as they were finally herded out of the arena.

"I never thought we'd make it out of that hell hole alive," she confessed.

Her toddler was still running a fever when they arrived in Texas. The three stayed at a small church in Dallas. There, Stephanie delivered her second child. Although the congregation surely did the very best they could, the space was small and privacy was nonexistent. Even more devastating, her husband became ill and died unexpectedly. Prompted by her father, the young mother and her two sons boarded a Greyhound bus for Detroit.

They all moved into her father's apartment, pretending to camp in the living room. She tucked the baby into a dresser drawer on the floor and her little boy used a sleeping bag. Their welcome was short-lived, though. When her father's girlfriend moved in, she insisted that the apartment wasn't big enough for two women. Stephanie's father dropped the trio off at the women's shelter in Highland Park. Then, the shelter was closed down.

Having survived the perfect storm in New Orleans, the premature death of her husband and the jealous demands of her father's friend, Stephanie was evicted from her fourth home—a homeless shelter. After listening to Stephanie's story, I was grateful for the luxury of two days notice and the generous friends who scrambled to help us assemble beds, mats, sheets, pillows, diapers and food for our new Family Shelter.

The ironic thing was that shortly after the government began relocating people following Hurricane Katrina, I got a call from a HUD staff member asking me how many people we could take in. I told the person that we were at capacity. The representative wasn't pleased with my answer. I made it clear that I would help if I could, but that forcing homeless people out to accommodate other homeless people didn't make sense to me. A lot of things still don't.

White Castle

No news may be good news but news coverage is a mixed bag. News stories shed light on the people and programs of organizations like Cass. Generally they deal with an individual or two to highlight what we do or what is needed for our program. Readers, listeners and viewers often respond with help. Sometimes this means material or financial donations. Being featured in a news story also alerts those who need assistance about where and how to get in touch with us. Almost every story that has ever included Cass has generated letters from prisoners. Once all three local news stations ran stories about the Cass Christmas Store, and we were overwhelmed by shoppers who simply showed up. We had prepared for 250 families but by the close of the day, after making multiple shopping trips of our own to restock the shelves, we had served 500 families. The next morning, 70 more people were lined up in front of the church at 8 a.m. We weren't even scheduled to operate the store a second day.

Very often people will call with requests after learning about our services. Following a newscast that included a piece about the extreme winter weather and our homeless outreach teams, the phone rang off the hook. People needed rides, shelter, food and assistance with utility shut-offs. Then, one person called on behalf of someone else: "Rev. Fowler, there is a man in the alley. His name is William Green. He used to be my neighbor. When his wife died last year, depression got the best of him. He quit his job and then he lost his house. The bank foreclosed on it. I'm afraid he's going to freeze to death."

Unfortunately, it's possible. One of the worst cases thought to be the result of the arctic cold in the last few years involved a man who was found at the bottom of an elevator shaft. His head, arms, trunk and upper legs were encased in a couple of feet of ice. His feet and legs below the knees stuck out. "Urban explorers" found him that way in the basement of what had been the Detroit Public Schools Book Repository. The young men played hockey near the man's corpse without notifying the police because they feared there would be legal consequences for trespassing.

"I'll send a team over to try and locate the man if you give me an address." She did and I did. It was five degrees outside, barely warm enough to walk to your car. I asked staffers Jeffery Eppes and Susan King to leave right away. They drove the van to the east side, plowed through a snow-covered alley and, just as the caller described, found her former neighbor next to the garage as cold and stationary as an ice sculpture. He was neither surprised nor frightened by the team. The three talked for about half an hour, but they returned to the Scott building alone.

I asked them where he was. Jeffery explained that although William was receptive to their visit, he was diametrically opposed to coming in to warm up. They attempted to woo him with the promise of warm food, a hot shower and clean clothes. "No," William told them, "I want to stay in my own neighborhood."

"Can you go back this afternoon?" I thought that as the sun set and the temperatures plunged even lower, he might be more receptive to coming in.

"Yeah. We'll head back at four o'clock."

By the time the pair had walked out of my office, the telephone rang again. It was the same concerned woman who had alerted us to William's predicament.

"I thought you said that you were sending someone out! What kind of minister are you?"

"Ma'am, we did go out. Actually, the team found William. He wasn't ready to come in but it's just a matter of time. We have to build up a relationship. It may take a couple of tries."

"He's gonna die out there."

"Ma'am, we can't make him come in," I stammered. "We aren't the police. William's not making good decisions, but he doesn't meet the standards to be involuntarily committed. It's not as easy as scooping up a stray dog. Our crew is going back this afternoon … "

Click.

Jeffery and Susan returned at the end of their shift. William was still slumped in the exact same place, as if tied there. The three talked some more. Susan handed him a cup of steaming coffee and then Jeffery directed the conversation to the loss of William's wife, how his grief probably initiated the downward spiral. The man listened and shook his head without saying anything.

Our two employees drove the six miles back to Scott once more without William. Disappointed. Worried. Afraid the caller might be right. Even if the extreme weather didn't take his life, we had to think about frostbite and hypothermia. "I'll call the police, but plan on making it your first stop in the morning, OK?" I added. "Let's get him in even if it's only for a couple hours. Promise him anything."

The dynamic duo headed out in the morning before I even made it into the office. This time they proved that they are my intellectual superiors. They stopped en route to pick up a secret weapon: a sack of White Castle hamburgers. The hamburgers, known colloquially as "sliders," are thin slabs of meat with holes similar to Swiss cheese. They're smothered with diced onion bits and topped off with mustard, ketchup and a couple of pickles. Jeffery jumped out of the van, handed William a coffee and two hamburgers. Without even sipping the hot drink, the malnourished man scarfed down the food.

"Did you like that?" Jeffery asked about the unconventional breakfast.

"Yes, it was good."

"Do you want some more?"

"You know I do."

"Help yourself, the rest are in the bag in the van."

William resembled a tortured "bait" dog used to train a pack of pit bulls as he slowly struggled to his feet. He braced himself with one hand on the garage wall, but it was evident that he was in physical distress. The staff members held his body up as William took the few excruciating steps to the van. They laid him on his side on the passenger's bench seat.

Once William was situated, Jeffery drove him directly to the nearest hospital. No passing Go. No collecting $200. There was no time to waste.

Hospitals aren't like they used to be. Twenty or 30 years ago, a woman would stay for a week to ten days after a normal birth. Today, it's just an overnight. The medical establishment has patients up and walking and out the door within a couple of days after a heart operation, hip replacement or brain surgery. William was admitted and sent straight from the emergency room to the ICU. He stayed in intensive care for two weeks before being transferred to a regular room. Six days later, the hospital was ready to discharge him, but he had nowhere to go. He remembered Jeffery and Susan and asked the hospital social worker to call Cass. This time without hamburgers, the team delivered him to the Scott Building.

It was a good thing they did. There was no way he could have handled the bandages and dressings that needed to be changed daily. He would have had difficulty on his own just monitoring and taking the pain medication prescribed. Our volunteer doctor, Sally Palmer, came in every day to provide the aftercare that William needed. He ended up living with us for 18 months. When he moved on, he had all of his fingers and toes and a wallet full of the telephone numbers that belonged to friends he planned to invite over to his new place.

A Tree Grows in Detroit

Samuel was diagnosed in 2005—the same year Cass opened Michigan's only residential program for homeless men with HIV/AIDS. His body had wasted away since he had received the diagnosis. He weighed in at just 100 pounds the day he arrived. What made him different from the 12 other men in the program, though, was that Samuel was a political refugee from Uganda.

His command of English was perfect. Samuel had a bachelor's degree and a keen intellect. Perhaps that's why he had a sense of entitlement. He felt that he deserved to be waited on and the remarkable thing is that the other men jumped at the chance. Tyrone voluntarily gave up his downstairs bedroom. Jimmy loaned Samuel his walker. Bill began to volunteer as Samuel's personal chef.

Or perhaps it was because his story was so compelling. This quiet 41-year-old celebrity told the others about leaving his wife and deserting their four children when he came to America. He talked about deep-rooted poverty and painted the picture of appalling brutality and torture. He said that if he went back home, he would certainly be killed. It was mind-blowing to the residents. None had ever set foot outside the United States. They couldn't imagine Samuel's life.

For reasons more pressing than politics, Samuel dared not be distracted by even illusions about going back home. He was extremely weak. Chronic nausea meant that he couldn't keep food or his cocktails of antiretroviral medications down. Even with Jimmy's walker, Samuel was unable to move the short distance fast enough to use the Jack and Jill bathroom.

One morning, Nate, a staff member, went to check on Samuel after breakfast. He found him curled up on the floor. Samuel was disoriented. His pants were wet with urine. Nate cleaned him up with the tender care of a nurse, changing his pants and underwear in the process. Then, he called for an ambulance before loading Samuel's stiff body into a wheelchair and rolling him down to the dining room. Bill fixed him some oatmeal and a cup of coffee. The EMS responders delivered our resident from East Africa to the closest hospital for treatment.

He died there three days later.

For two years we had been telling the men at Cass House that they could live to see middle or even old age. They had watched so many of their friends and partners experience cruel, premature deaths. They had expected to die themselves once diagnosed. They quit jobs, gave away their belongings and planned their own funerals in an attempt to save their families or friends from the task. We preached to them that that was the past. AIDS was a treatable disease now. No, it hadn't been cured and, yes, there were side effects from the drugs, but they could grow old and complain about bad knees and deteriorating hips and failing eyesight like the rest of us.

Then Samuel died. A pall hung over the house. Our emotions seesawed between love and loss. I suspected that the men were watching to see how we would mark Samuel's life. Each worried about his own demise and whether anyone would take notice. We decided to plant a tree on the property in Samuel's memory. It would live longer than any of the residents or staff who gathered around it for a simple memorial service. Many mourners spoke that day about our charmer from Uganda—what made him unique, why his friendship was important, how his passing could challenge residents to stop taking medication sporadically. Each resident signed up for a shift to water the young tree.

By the time Cass took over Michigan's only housing for women and children with AIDS in 2012, people in our country had begun to think of the disease as they did about diabetes—it was something manageable. Individuals with AIDS could just pop a few pills was the thought. Gone was the urgency of prevention education. Few were focused on finding a cure. Celebrities had shifted their attention from dying or living with AIDS to same-sex marriage as if we could only deal with one social issue at a time. Of course, there is never that luxury in a poor or minority community. At Cass, we keep planting trees.

Hey Ms. Tambourine Woman

The Wednesday night worship is strictly voluntarily. Residents, volunteers, staff members and community people gather in the warehouse to sing, pray and listen to an abbreviated sermon delivered by a visiting clergyperson. Folding chairs are arranged between lawn equipment and recycling bins. Cee Cee always claims a seat at the end of an aisle. Worship starts when she rattles her tambourine.

She doesn't belong to the choir. In fact, occasionally the choir director shoots her a disapproving look in the hopes that it will cause her to sit down. No matter. Cee Cee is on her feet with a jerky, high-stepping march movement, crashing one hand against the tambourine and then shooting it into the air as if she is a drum major.

She has come a long way. More than half of her adult life she was homeless, jumping from shelter to shelter until she ended up at Mom's Place. She exceeded the time limit there and moved into another agency until there was a renovated unit in the Brady Building. While she was gone, the Cass PATH team helped her obtain social security benefits. Although she was undiagnosed for 50 years, Cee Cee is bipolar, has long suffered with addiction and has a history of seizures.

Her first seizure occurred when she was 15. Standing at the stove, Cee Cee fell to the floor, knocking a pot and its boiling contents down on top of her in the process. Scars from the third degree burns are still evident on her face, hands, arms and legs. She is certain that they make her unattractive, although most people don't notice because they become absorbed by her constant chatter. She is hyper-verbal and her conversation is rife with religious references like "Jesus gonna help me."

Cee Cee would know. When she was 16, her parents divorced. Pregnant, she dropped out of school during 10th grade to get married. Cee Cee miscarried twins at 19. She and her husband did their best to raise two boys and a girl. Their marriage ended after 17 years when her husband died. Her mother passed when Cee Cee was just 30 years old. Her alcohol, weed and crack cocaine habits cost Cee Cee her children, and the next 25 years of her life.

To see her singing and playing at the evening service, you'd never know any of it. She is punctual, congenial and well-groomed. Occasionally she'll share her concerns about her neighbors at the Brady Building. She runs errands for the seniors. She shares food with those who haven't managed their money well. Being homeless taught Cee Cee to squirrel away her cash. She'll tell you that it's easy now because she doesn't have any vices. "I don't smoke. I don't drink. I don't gamble," she says. And then she adds her personal motto, "If it's not sold at the dollar store, I don't need it."

Her case manager helped her establish a savings account rather than keep her riches between the mattresses. That was when the trouble began. The Social Security Administration, which gives her $698 a month to live on, sent her a letter indicating that she had too much money in her account. A person receiving SSI can have only $2,000 to his or her name.

Our staff talked with her about purchasing something: new furniture, a big-screen TV, a vacation, a bicycle, a new wardrobe. Cee Cee indicated that she was content with what she had and that she wanted to save the money in case of an emergency. After more prodding, she finally bought herself a bike, a used bike.

Six months later, another official letter arrived, again questioning why she had saved up over $2,000. Convinced that she was going to lose her income by friends and family members with questionable motives, Cee Cee decided to withdraw her money from the bank and hide it in her bed once more.

An unnamed staff member persuaded Cee Cee that there was a better way to stay ready for that "rainy day." After being educated about all the logistics, she went to her bank and opened a safe-deposit box. What she put in there, I couldn't tell you. Only Cee Cee and Jesus know what she socked away in the vault. The bank records confirm that her savings account has less than $2,000.

Open Meetings

Every year brings virgin members to the Cass board of directors. The agency bylaws stipulate that board members can serve no more than six consecutive years, meaning there is a constant rotation of people. Every January meeting involves getting to know the newcomers and helping them become familiar with Cass activities and affairs. Often it means overcoming culture shock. We are fortunate enough to enlist individuals from the top tier of several corporate ladders—the CEOs and other executives from banks, hospitals and the auto industry. We regularly have partners from some of the best legal firms and owners of area small businesses. They bring expertise that we couldn't pay for, but there is a learning curve for most because they generally haven't been exposed to poverty or people who are attempting to escape it.

One January board meeting was probably 20 minutes into the agenda items when a knock at the door interrupted the session. The intruding staff member explained that there were two women in the front hallway who were asking about the "stockholder" meeting. Perplexed by the question and thinking that everyone had arrived, I excused myself to see who it was and why they had come. Standing together, checking out the bulletin board, were resident Tereasa and her friend Riley. "Can I help you?" I asked.

"We're here for the stockholders' meeting," Tereasa said, pointing to the laminated poster with the board member photos and the annual meeting schedule.

"Oh, you mean the board meeting?" I corrected her.

"Yeah," she said. "They are open meetings, aren't they?" Tereasa could be described as disgruntled on good days. She almost always had a laundry list of grievances and suggested repairs.

"Yes, they are," I said while thinking that it wasn't a good night for visitors. "Follow me."

Staff member Stacy Leigh was halfway through her annual Continuous Quality Improvement presentation when the two women sat down at the table. Tereasa seated herself in one swooping motion while her companion dramatically pulled a chair across the carpet and re-positioned it multiple times before plopping down with a thud. She then asked for all the available written reports for the meeting. Riley rifled through the paperwork, highlighting sentences and whole paragraphs with the yellow marker that she had taken out of her purse.

When Stacy paused for questions from board members, Tereasa seized on the opportunity to filibuster. "You don't know me, but I live in the Wesley Building." I half expected her to pull out an Excel spreadsheet at this point to read off her complaints. Surprisingly, she didn't gripe about anything.

She continued, "You can't begin to understand the life I have lived. My father was a pedophile. He started having sex with me when I was 6 years old. I turned to drugs at 14 because I just couldn't take it any longer. Then, I ran away from home.

"Somehow, I managed to complete college with honors, but I had a nervous breakdown after the graduation ceremony. School had been my entire life for four years; and suddenly I didn't have anywhere to go.

"I got a job driving a cab in Columbus. But old habits die hard. My drug use increased, and I began cheating with credit cards. It cost me. I did a year in Marysville. Nine months of that time was spent in solitary."

The room went quiet, like when you submerge underwater. I've read that 'fear not' is spoken 366 times in the Bible, enough for every day of the year even if it's a leap year; still I worried that the newest members of the governing body might be questioning their decisions to serve. I translated their silence to mean that they had never met anyone who had served time, much less in solitary confinement.

"Once I got out, I had a year clean but still I didn't have a place to stay. I started working in a psych ward, where one of the other employees was selling crack. I started using again.

"Next, I became involved in a check ring, writing bad checks. This time I went to federal prison. In 2012, I was paroled and living in a transitional housing program for federal prisoners."

All of a sudden I remembered the movie title, *They Shoot Horses, Don't They?*

Tereasa, just kill me now, I thought.

"When my time ended, once more, I didn't have anywhere to go. I called 1-800-SHELTER and they referred me to the Cass Warming Center. I got a mat by the window grill so I could pull myself up because I was obese by then. I weighed 450 pounds. From there, I got into the Rotating Shelter and then into Mom's Place.

"I stopped using illegal drugs and started taking medication for bipolar disorder in 2012 because I was finally diagnosed. Clean and sober, I moved into the Wesley House building. It was rough at first. I was in trouble off and on with the staff because I let old friends in who probably stole stuff."

I recalled the missing fire extinguishers, the construction tools, the lawnmower …

"I had trouble just getting up and down the stairs to my apartment on the second floor.

"Then, in March of 2013, I had bariatric bypass surgery. And you know what? Gloria, my case manager, came to see me in the hospital and at the rehabilitation facility. I couldn't believe it. I had been such a pain in the neck.

"I've lost 110 pounds since then. I still have more to lose but nothing is going to stop me now. I go to water aerobics. I serve on the Family Advisory Council. I sponsor four women in NA. I go to church. I've just been accepted into the Social Work School at Wayne State University."

"Tell them what NA is," I interjected.

"Narcotics Anonymous," Tereasa blurted out. She had no idea that some people would be unfamiliar with the acronym.

"So here's what I came to say. This is our community. It's taken me and others a lifetime to get here. We don't take it for granted and we're not going to tolerate drugs or crime or sexual predators here. And you should know this, too … Rev. Fowler isn't done. She's got a vision. I told her last week at Warehouse Worship, 'You need to keep going. We'll be behind you. This community saved my life.'"

No one quit the board. Tereasa, in fact, had made my job so much easier. Now, when board members hear about prisoner re-entry or substance abuse recovery or surviving sexual abuse or the need for community mental health, they see Tereasa's face and hear her voice—its pain and its pride. And they remember that their work is critical because men, women and children deserve a safe, affordable and nurturing community.

Twice Tereasa went into inpatient rehab following the board session. Both times she returned to Cass and relapsed. She used illegal narcotics and sold them. Her behavior and those of her dealing visitors became increasingly loud and disruptive. Other building residents feared for their safety, as did the staff members. We were forced to evict Tereasa. It's not how we want her story to end. We can only remind ourselves that it's not over yet.

CHAPTER 5

Jobs

Million-Dollar Sofa

John Maxwell writes that a shark's size is determined by its tank. In other words, held captive in a five- or 10-gallon aquarium, a shark will remain stunted and small. Relocate the same fish to a hundred gallon container and it will grow larger, but not to its natural adult size. Liberate the shark by releasing it in the ocean and it will grow to 20, 30, 40 feet depending on the species.

I don't know if Maxwell is correct but I do subscribe to a proportionate theory. The more space available at Cass, the more stuff we collect. We religiously fill every room and building to capacity. When the agency moved into the 30,000-square-foot Scott Building in 2002, it felt as if we had transitioned from a small starter home into the 250-room Biltmore Estate. There were so many bathrooms and community spaces. And for the first time, we had access to bedrooms and multiple staff offices. The entire basement was yet to be renovated, but when it was finished, the new commercial kitchen was three times larger than the one we had used in the church. Yet, within two years, every possible nook, cranny and cupboard was occupied.

When the opportunity came up for us to purchase the warehouse across the street from the Scott Building in 2007, we jumped at the chance. This added 10,000 more square feet, and we were eager to have a location to receive, sort, display and distribute donations. People needed clothing, appliances, furniture, household items like pots and pans, silverware and bedding. The cavernous warehouse allowed us to arrange the things so that people could come in and select what they needed and liked.

Back to the proportionate theory. Every day people would call the Cass switchboard and request furniture donation pickups. Our driver would schedule appointments for the transfer of property. He would secure the old box truck and arrange for a jumper for each trip. A jumper was necessary because the furnishings were heavy and clunky and usually situated on at least the third floor of an elevator-impaired apartment building. The two would follow the directions on a Google map to reach the destinations. Occasionally, the truck would have a flat tire or lose a muffler or the duo would fail to pay attention to a low-hanging bridge (thus ripping off the box roof of the truck so that it appeared as if it had been attacked by a gigantic can opener). But generally speaking, pickups happened without incident and frequently enough so that the warehouse soon looked as if it belonged on an episode of A&E's *Hoarders*.

Geneal Martin and I went one day to pick up a million-dollar sofa. By-the-by, every city pastor should get a commercial driver's license as soon as she or he is appointed. The truck was in rare form—the windshield was severely cracked, the air-conditioning was dead and, consequently, we had to travel with the windows down. If it hadn't been so hot, we certainly would have kept them closed to muffle the sound. Someone had stolen the catalytic converter the night before. The cube truck sounded like a Harley Davidson rally. Not a problem, we were just going to a gated community in an affluent suburb. Moreover, the truck's top speed was 50 mph, and thus we enjoyed the afternoon together as other drivers gave us hand signs and verbal blessings on the expressway.

We pulled into the circular drive and loaded up a couple of rooms of furniture before the donor mentioned her couch in the basement. Geneal was young and brawny, but even he was perspiring profusely. We descended into a man-cave area where the woman told us that the sofa was worth a great deal of money. She continued saying that, although it hadn't been used in several years, it was in good condition as long as you covered it with a sheet or blanket.

We squatted down at opposite armrests and grunted as we lifted the luxurious antique off the floor. The million-dollar sofa was a substantial sofa bed. It weighed as much as a couple of sumo wrestlers Velcroed together. My eyes were watering as we tilted the bulky beast to start up the stairwell. I could feel my legs throbbing. Finally, dripping wet, we squeezed the sofa into the remaining gap in the cargo area.

While I was rolling the garage-like door down, the woman inched up next to me and said: "You're not going to sell my things, are you? That's why I don't give to the Salvation Army. They charge needy people for the things that were given to them. I don't think it's right. You don't do that, do you?" She talked a mile-a-minute and I was still trying to breathe. I probably should have defended the Salvation Army. We partner with them all the time and they do good work, but I didn't. I assured her that no one had to pay for things at Cass.

Hers was not a million-dollar sofa because it was constructed of mahogany wood or fine Italian leather. Under the cover, we didn't discover silk tassels hanging from the bottom. Hers was an ordinary 1950s functional sleeper sofa. No, its value came in helping me re-think what it costs to give away a sofa.

First, you have to have a motor vehicle. Buying a used one costs at least $5,000 or $6,000. Unfortunately, we have learned that the cheaper the truck, the more regular and more expensive the repairs. You must then purchase a license, insurance and gasoline for the vehicle that gets eight to 12 miles per gallon. Then, there has to be a driver who must be credentialed, responsible and congenial with strangers. Next you need someone to ride shotgun, a jumper who has have the strength of Samson to be able to lift chest freezers and grand pianos and Prohibition-era safes as well as sofas.

Then, of course, you must store the furniture. We bought a foreclosed warehouse. Even though the building is managed by volunteers, there are operational expenses. It costs a small fortune to insure, heat and light the space. The building requires cleaning supplies for the bathrooms, exterminator services and monitoring for the security system, as well as random facility repairs.

Finally, after the shoppers select a sofa, they need help getting it home. Fifty percent of Detroiters and 99.9 percent of people who are homeless don't own a car, much less a truck. And have you tried taking a sofa on a city bus lately? So Cass incurs all the truck, driver, jumper and gasoline expenses once again to deliver the second-hand furniture. It hit me like a ton of ottomans—there's no such thing as a free lunch or a free sofa.

Geneal completed the contribution form so the woman would have documentation of her donation for tax purposes and then we started back to the warehouse in our rumbling, rickety truck. The gas tank was on empty.

South Detroit

Journey sings a great line in the song "Don't Stop Believing." It says that a city boy was "born and raised in south Detroit." The lyric is a dead giveaway that the song writer wasn't from here. There is no south Detroit. South Detroit is Windsor, Canada.

The other missing thing that surprises outsiders about Detroit—jobs. They can't believe the Motor City has changed so dramatically. Ever since Henry Ford introduced the assembly line and established a $5-a-day wage in the 1940s, huge waves of people were lured to the city from southern states for jobs. Immigrants from Poland, Germany, Belgium, Lithuania and Hungary came for work, too. They didn't need to speak English. They didn't need a diploma. They weren't required to have a skill. Thanks to strong labor unions, job applicants were taken in and trained within an hour or so, and if they made it past the 90-day probationary period, the new hires were propelled into America's middle class. But over time, automotive jobs disappeared like water under the scorching Sahara sun.

As the city's older manufacturing plants became obsolete, they were shut down–Packard Motor, Hudson Motor, Studebaker, the Briggs Body plants and the Clark Avenue plant. New facilities were built in the suburbs, like Warren and Woodhaven where land was available for the buildings and immense parking lots. Then the car companies relocated to the southern states, like Alabama and Georgia, where unions didn't have a stronghold. Finally, they moved to foreign countries where the labor and legacy costs were a small percentage of those in the United States. By the 1990s, an adult had a better chance at being admitted into Julliard than landing an entry-level automotive job in Detroit.

Other large and small employers were also eliminated or transplanted to the suburbs after the 1967 riot. The urban rebellion had been in response to discrimination by law enforcement—Detroit had a near all-white police department—and the brutal tactics of the STRESS unit, in particular. Businesses were looted. A number were burned to the ground. The National Guard was brought in to end the havoc. At the conclusion of the riots, white residents and businesses left the city— physically and emotionally. The jobs went with them.

Getting to distant jobs proved a formative task for those living in Detroit. Since next to none of the homeless people in our programs had vehicles, transportation was a major problem. Those without transportation were forced to walk great distances from the end of the city bus line to their places of employment. People of color with cars were routinely stopped by suburban law enforcement.

Transportation wasn't the only obstacle to employment though. Automation made unskilled workers redundant and application requirements more stringent. Large numbers of homeless men and women lacked a high school diploma or even a GED. A few were illiterate. Many didn't have a decent work history or current references. Moreover, they couldn't provide a permanent address or a direct telephone number. Some were eliminated from consideration due to their criminal records. Others couldn't pass a drug test. Over time, employers even started requiring credit checks. Homeless individuals rarely have FICO scores above 750.

The case managers at Cass worked diligently to identify employers who would hire homeless individuals for even seasonal or part-time positions. They reached out to agency alumni for leads. Every time there was a job fair, our social workers would load up a bus full of resume-ready searchers to participate. The lunchroom bulletin boards were plastered with employment notices. We did all right making the connections. Our people became painters, security guards, custodians, movers, stockers and waitresses, until the economy collapsed in southeastern Michigan in late 2007, well before the rest of the country experienced the recession. At that point in time, we couldn't get work for a member of Mensa.

Thus, we made the decision to convert the Cass warehouse from a distribution center to an employment building. The reasoning was that our agency could refer people to other outlets for beds and dressers, tables and chairs. There were also a number of outstanding organizations which could provide clothing, coats, boots, etc. Although folks could receive superior job training elsewhere, when they were finished they were right back where they started—unemployed.

Before creating permanent employment, Cass dabbled with smaller piece assignments which provided work. We wrapped printed materials. We assembled popcorn envelopes on display boards. Probably our most notable short-term employment project was catnip. Temporary staff assisted by volunteers weighed and packaged pallets full of the smelly, hallucinogenic leaves in small clear plastic baggies. It was always a bit of a mystery why we weren't raided. Just about every youth group took pictures of the operation and often we spotted the shots posted on the Internet. It sure looked as if we were assembling 5-gram bags of weed. Occasionally, people would sneak out samples, but only their cats were getting high.

Eventually, I reached the conclusion that we needed to start a self-sustaining business of our own in order to provide ongoing jobs. I wanted the work to be linked to the environment because poor communities are hit hardest and first by environmental degradation. My proof of this theory was southwest Detroit.

The southwest section of the city stands in stark contrast to much of the rest of Detroit. Southwest has some of the best kept properties in Detroit. The lawns are manicured and accented with trimmed bushes and fragrant rose gardens. Vernor Highway and other commercial streets are healthy and colorful with beautiful murals. Blocks are jam-packed with great Mexican restaurants and stores. The neighborhood is teeming with people. The population, mostly but not exclusively Hispanic, is growing. The only problem in southwest Detroit is breathing.

When returning home by car from anywhere south of the city, you drive north on I-75 and the expressway takes you right through southwest Detroit. It is smack dab in the middle of Michigan's most polluted zip code. No one needs to consult scientific research or even an EPA report to verify this. Travelers have a visceral reaction to the rancid odors that waft through their windows. At 65 miles per hour, you will see multiple industrial chimneys billowing thick smoke. Even if visibility is poor or your eyes are watering, you won't be able to miss one of the heavy, dusty trucks hauling cement, asphalt, steel or oil as it enters the freeway.

The amazing thing about southwest Detroit isn't that it is part of a regular "Toxic Tour" of the city, but that roughly 9,000 people live in close proximity to the bridge. Scores of them are long-time residents. Nearly everyone has health issues that they attribute to the polluted air, water and land. Remember William, Chandra's son with all the food allergies? He has debilitating asthma. It is so severe that he makes six to eight trips to the emergency room every year, gasping for breath like a fish frantically flopping on the deck of a boat. Chandra has asthma, too. So does William's sister and his aunt. Others talk about living or dying with various types of cancer. Why do they live in southwest Detroit? They relish the people, the culture, the attractive community and how much money could they get for their house?

Green Industries was born first as the idea that we could marry two urban problems—unemployment and pollution—and create a solution which would change the odds for everybody.

You Know You Are
Home When

Returning to Detroit from Metro Airport, you know you are home when you pass the gigantic tire on I-94 in Allen Park. Illuminated, it stands out even at night, as I imagine it did as part of an 8-story Ferris wheel in the 1964 New York World's Fair. The gondolas were removed and a tread installed in their place when the tire arrived in Michigan. Beyond that, there have only been a few minor changes over the years—a new hub cap was installed, Uniroyal's name and web address were added and, temporarily, a 500-pound nail was attached. But the treads are deep and the black rubber never went flat. Metropolitan Detroiters tend to see the mammoth tire as a symbol of the local automotive industry's might.

When you drive into the city proper, you know you are home when you pass not one, but numerous illegally dumped tires. They litter almost every neighborhood. They are scattered two or three deep on a curb or vacant lot. In some spots, they are piled higher than your head. It is not uncommon to see a few hundred, heaped helter-skelter like an urban mountain. In the city, tires are not a symbol of strength, but of blight and scurrilous activity.

Pickup trucks snake along the city's side streets in the middle of the night and unidentifiable people toss the tires out of the rolling vehicles. Brazen box trucks do the same, dumping their heavy loads, without even bothering to hide the signs that bear their company names. Tire crimes require sentencing reform. Convicted violators should have a "T" tattooed on their foreheads. The consequence must be stiff because, more often than not, two crimes have been committed. Generally, a trusting customer has paid a recycling fee to an unscrupulous businessperson who pockets the cash and then arranges to illegally dispose of the old tires. Perhaps instead of the "T," people convicted of participating in illegal dumping should have to live surrounded by discarded tires without the possibility of removal. You can determine if the punishment fits the crime or if it is a little harsh. Picture waking up tomorrow and discovering that your front lawn has been covered not with pink flamingoes planted by your friends as a prank, but with used tires dropped off by strangers who are never coming back to retrieve them. Catching the scoundrels is a rarity. Most of the streetlights don't work, and the police are preoccupied with felonies.

It won't take you long to conclude that tires never make for good neighbors. They are unsightly. They are heavy and grimy and costly to clean up. If you don't dispose of them, their curves will collect rainwater, and they become breeding grounds for mosquitoes in the summer. Rodents reproduce in them the rest of the year. Moving mounds of tires to cut the grass each week is an impossibility. What's more, tires retain heat and can easily ignite. Occasionally, someone deliberately sets a pile on fire. Then, you will discover that tires are stubborn and hard to extinguish. Burning tires fill the air and your lungs with poison.

One day, I read an article about a new cottage industry in Oklahoma that recycled tires into doormats. Given the infinite supply of illegally dumped tires in Detroit and the desperate need for jobs, I reached out to the agency that works with

Native American people, most of them of the Cherokee tribe. "Would you tell me how you got started with the doormats and how the business is doing?" I asked.

The gentleman on the other end of the phone was extremely generous with information and his time. Their employment program sounded like a perfect fit for what I wanted to start in Michigan. I threw my caution to the wind after he was finished.

"We stole your land," I said, "How would you feel about us permanently borrowing your idea?" (I've always believed that it's best to start with confession.) Fortunately, he laughed. Then, he graciously provided all the details necessary for replicating the mat program.

An anonymous donor provided the $4,000 needed for startup. The funds allowed us to purchase a saw and punch, some wire and spacers. Ten men, homeless and formerly homeless, were hired to make Cass mud mats from discarded tires. Since the program's inception, up to a dozen men have worked in the Cass program without interruption. All of their wages have been covered by mud mat sales.

In 2009, Magic Johnson served as the honorary chair at a Cass fundraiser. The program manager asked if one of the workers would make a mat in Michigan State colors to be presented to Magic at the event. Albert volunteered. He set up wires in his workstation. Then he painstakingly selected the pre-punched strips of rubber, collected enough green and white spacers, and finally he wove the wires, rubber strips and spacers into a perfect mat. When he was done clamping the ends, Albert attached a metal Cass logo tag on the front before he flipped it over. We thought he was to hoist up the mat to show off his work. Instead, he signed his name to the back of the mat using a silver Sharpie permanent marker. No one had ever done that before. Since that day, all of the workers have repeated the act of signing the mats they create.

Thousands of volunteers help us gather illegally dumped tires. We call the collection process "tire hunting," but no hounds or weapons are required. An empty truck and a passenger van go out together. Sometimes the search is random, meaning the team just drives until they find enough raw materials to fill the truck. At other times, neighbors, community groups, government offices or even news stations will alert us to particular areas that are rich in illegally dumped bounty. Either way, the repurposed rubber has helped us marry reducing poverty and protecting the planet. The hunters and laborers turn blocks of unsightly blight into an attractive, environmentally friendly Detroit product of which both groups are proud.

The White House

"Would you be willing to speak at the White House?" the caller inquired.

Did she say the White House? It must have been the jailhouse, the doghouse, the outhouse ...

"Huh?" I responded, because I have two master's degrees.

"It's the anniversary of McKinney-Vento and the Faith and Community-Based Partnerships to End Homelessness will be hosting a roundtable. Would you be willing to sit on a panel for the White House event?" McKinney-Vento is the Housing and Urban Development funding for programs that serve people who are homeless and mentally ill.

"Let me check my schedule." I ruffled a few papers loudly so the caller would think I was actually reviewing a calendar. Who knew where my Franklin planner was? "Yep, I'm free."

I quickly booked an early morning flight because I was teaching the night before and the Washington conference didn't start until 3 p.m. That day, I arrived at the airport on time (which is not always the case), made my way through the long security lines (no small feat with a mud mat in tow) and then sat down in the waiting area by the flight's gate. People were talking obnoxiously loud into their cell phones. CNN was rehashing the news on several mounted television screens.

The monitor behind the desk listed the many departure times until silently it swapped. My flight changed to 'delayed.'

"No," I had flown enough and read enough Langston Hughes to know what happens to a plane deferred.

"There's got to be another flight," my words rose in a crescendo.

"I have to get to Washington right away," I wailed at the 20-something man behind the nearest Delta counter.

"That's not gonna happen," he responded, shaking his head as if I didn't understand English.

"The only other plane to D.C. this morning leaves in 20 minutes," … meaning there is no possible way you can make the trip.

"That's plenty of time," I responded, "book me on it."

He hammered away on the computer keys, wasting at least four of my available minutes and handed me a paper boarding pass, as was the custom back then. I sprinted through the station like O.J. Simpson in the old Avis commercials.

My plane landed at Dulles International Airport rather than Reagan National (where my luggage arrived). I caught a cab to the hotel because all of a sudden I was worried about time. The fare from the alternate airport was $90. I combed my hair, added a little make-up and walked the half-mile to the White House complex. It was a little intimidating at the security gate. Of course, I had submitted paperwork well in advance to obtain a special clearance. Still, the officers checked my identification and everyone was scanned with a metal detector. A small group of us waited together, and then we were escorted up to the presentation room in the government building next to the White House.

Four panelists made presentations and answered questions from both the facilitator, Philip Mangano, and members of the audience. It went OK. I didn't run into the commander in chief (I had hoped to present him with the mud mat) and so, when we were finished, I walked back to the hotel, mud mat in hand, stopping only to grab some Mexican food for dinner.

I changed from my business attire to the sweat suit that I had stuffed into my carry-on, and started enjoying the vegetarian burrito and Diet Coke.

Wait a minute, where's my driver's license? I asked myself, digging through my pockets and purse. I couldn't believe that I'd lost my ID! It's got to be back by the White House. Without finishing my meal, I dashed back to the security booth. The shift must have changed because I didn't recognize anyone from the last visit. "Can I help you?" an armed guard asked.

"I hope so," I said. "I think I left my driver's license inside."

His eyes shot up and down my sweat suit as if to say "Sure."

"Really," I pleaded, "I was a presenter at the conference this afternoon." I wondered how many times he had had to deal with people trying to get inside.

"Wait here," he put me out of the booth on the wrong side of the gate. Then he disappeared into the building.

I began working myself up into a panic. "What am I going to do? I have to be back at work tomorrow. I have a speaking engagement tomorrow night. They're not even going to let me board the plane in the morning."

I don't know if the guard heard me talking to myself, he didn't say. "You must be mistaken," he declared. "We checked the room and there's no license anywhere."

I walked back to the hotel a second time, pensively, deliberately, with my head down to look for the license along the way and to avoid looking anyone in the eye. It wasn't on the sidewalk and it wasn't in the Mexican restaurant. I checked. I was crushed.

I had been so excited to come to the conference and now it looked as if I'd never get home. I asked for a ridiculously early wake-up call. I knew that I'd better get to the airport before the sun rose. The cab dropped me at Dulles at 6:30 a.m. I stood in line with business people who were undoubtedly traveling to executive meetings. The TSA officer asked for my identification. I handed over my photo ID from the University of Michigan.

"You don't have identification with your address?" he barked.

"I left my license at the White House," I replied.

He didn't crack a smile. Maybe he's heard that line before.

"No, really," I continued. "I was here for the McKinney-Vento anniversary roundtable. I work with homeless people in Detroit. I was a presenter. Anyway, I had to have my driver's license to get into the White House grounds. I must have left it in there, but they couldn't find it … "

I don't know why he let me through. Maybe he just wanted to watch Bertha give me a hard time. I placed my carry-on and the mud mat on the moving belt. She stopped it before it reached the x-ray machine. "You can't take that on the plane," she grabbed my mud mat.

"I took it past White House security," I said, not bothering to distinguish which building.

This huge Neanderthal woman yanked me out of the line and shook me like a dog shakes a rat. Then through my dirty sweat suit, she examined most of my body cavities in front of perfect strangers. Not one for public displays, I was extremely relieved when she finally let me pass.

I rescued my mud mat—she was going to have to fight me for it at that point—and I went leaping and dancing all through the terminal like David bringing the Ark into Jerusalem. I took two mat orders on the way to my gate. The flight home was uneventful except for a little turbulence before we landed at Metro.

The next problem was that I was slated to take a bunch of youth to Texas that weekend. We were going to fly and I was supposed to drive the rental car but I still didn't have a license. There wasn't even enough time to have one reissued through the Secretary of State. So I used a passport to board the plane and asked one of the other adults to handle the ground transportation. We were in Texas, making P.E.T.—personal energy transportation—carts for people who had lost mobility due to land mines or diseases like polio, when my cell phone rang. The screen read 'unknown' caller.

"Hello," I took the chance that it wasn't somebody wanting to sell me a timeshare.

"Faith Fowler?"

"That's me. Can I help you?"

"This is John Smith from the security staff at the White House," the caller answered. "I have your driver's license."

"Oh, good," I exclaimed, relieved on so many levels. "Thank God."

"I'll mail it to you," he said. "What's your address?"

Next time you have to take off your shoes, belt and jacket at the airport, lift up a prayer for the safety of the sitting president.

Liabilities

Forty-four dollars is the monthly income for people living in AFC homes. It is true that their housing and food is paid for, but everything else must come out of the $44 state check. This includes their clothing, transportation, recreation, medication co-pays, personal hygiene items, birthday celebrations and holiday gifts. It's just not enough money. Thus, it is imperative for these men and women to have another source of income.

When the economy is strong, some are employed in fast-food restaurants and retail businesses, and many have jobs in sheltered workshops. Employees in sheltered workshops do piece work with other developmentally disabled adults like assembling small parts, packaging products or tagging items. Although the sheltered workshops provide jobs, workers earn deviated wages, meaning their compensation can range from prevailing rates to less than $1 per hour. When the economy tanks, working people with developmental disabilities tend to be negatively impacted before others. Starting in late 2007, Michigan experienced a financial crisis that generally reduced the hours or eliminated the jobs for these adults. Moreover, securing new positions for them was about as likely as having a meteor land on your house.

Thus, we began exploring ideas for a new business that could employ them with at least minimum wages. The mud mats were selling so well that we were starting the men at slightly more than the minimum wage. Perhaps, we thought, Cass could develop something similar for adults with developmental disabilities. In fact, we knew from the Activity Center program that these men and women would be exceptional employees. They had both an incredible work ethic and stellar attendance records. Most were highly motivated to please others, and so many of the common teamwork problems wouldn't plague a business set up for these folks. The difficult issue in designing a business was that the majority of the adults were permanently illiterate.

Then … eureka! Former Board Chair Barry Waldman introduced me to his friend Greg Bereznoff, who introduced me to his brother-in-law Bob Chadwick, who was the chief executive officer of Tuscola Behavioral Health Systems before he took over as CEO of Cass Valley Enterprises. CVE is a manufacturing business in Vassar, Michigan that employs people with disabilities. Bob helped me realize that their greatest liability could also be their greatest asset. Cass could start a document destruction business: our men and women would be the perfect employees because they couldn't read, write, remember or tell the confidential information that people wanted to be destroyed—Social Security numbers, patient information, addresses and so on. In addition to installing surveillance cameras and alarm systems, we could promise our customers supreme security because the employees had no idea what they were shredding.

We just needed two things to start the business: customers and shredding equipment. Staff members contacted friends who were lawyers and doctors and accountants and asked them to provide paper with sensitive information for shredding. Then, after mounting security cameras that met IRS standards, we purchased three small shredding machines. You know, the Staples or Office Depot variety with baby teeth that fit on the top of wastebaskets. Could the employees handle the job? Would they like it? How long would the shredding take?

We hired five people. They worked in a 15- by 25-foot room with the three modest office machines, some tables and chairs. Two people removed large paper clips and took the materials out of binders while the other three inserted the small stacks of documents into the shredders. Even though they were only inserting three to five sheets at once, the equipment jammed quite often and the small bins needed to be emptied about every half hour. Still, the new hires were happy, especially on payday. Sheila danced with her check. George didn't dance, but every day thereafter he split open his wallet to display the dollar bills tucked inside for everyone he met. When visitors asked these workers what they enjoyed most about their jobs, every one of them made the unofficial money sign by rubbing the fingers and thumb together. It took the group a year and a half to shred a ton of paper, yet it was more than a ton that would be recycled.

Next, we were able to obtain mid-sized commercial-grade shredding machines. Each was able to destroy 15 to 18 sheets of paper simultaneously. The larger machines didn't jam quite so much, although they drank oil by the gallon. We moved the operation into a larger room and marketed the shredding services beyond our friends. Who knew that lawyers were such hoarders? Our staff picked up truckloads of files, computer paper and journals. Twenty more employee shredders were engaged. This group and the new equipment could shred a ton of paper every four weeks.

As the weeks went by, the new workers appeared for their shifts with candy and pop. They came wearing new shoes, baseball hats and wristwatches. Steve liked to ask people to look at his timepiece. "Do you like my watch?" he'd inquire of everyone touring the warehouse.

"Absolutely," "Definitely," "You bet." People universally answered in the affirmative.

"What time does it say?" he'd ask.

His watch didn't have a digital display. After the guest told him the time, Steve would ask, "Is that the right time?"

If not, he would unbuckle the strap and pass his watch off so that the hands could be reset to the correct time. Once he secured it back on his wrist, Steve would smile and ask one last question, "Now how do you like my watch?"

Things were humming. The business picked up additional customers—a trucking company, a school system, some more lawyers and doctors. Then, we entered an online competition to win a quarter of a million dollars. It was a long shot. Eleven thousand organizations registered from all over the country. Cass staff and volunteers were cornered to vote, and the campaign occurred during our United Methodist Detroit Annual Conference, so we were able to urge a good number of United Methodists to take part in the contest, using four borrowed iPads supported by several of the younger clergy members. When the voting concluded, Cass was in the top 100 nonprofits, and so we moved on to round two.

For a second time, we telephoned, faxed, emailed, messaged friends on Facebook and stopped total strangers in Starbucks to get votes. For three solid weeks, we did everything but pole dance to try and win. It wasn't enough, though. We finished in 36th place. Sure, the social networking didn't hurt us, but staff members and even some of the residents felt defeated and heartbroken. Days later, we received word that the contest's advisory committee had selected Cass' shredding business concept as one of the best ideas in the country, and Chase Bank awarded the agency $68,000.

We bought industrial equipment with the prize money. No longer were the men and women shredding paper. Do you remember the *I Love Lucy* episode where Lucy and Ethel work at the candy factory? Our shredders became sorters along a similar 20-foot conveyor belt. Derrick was promoted to line leader. He assumed the job of dumping the contents from the 65-gallon locking containers at one end of the strip, and the other employees were assigned spots along the belt culling out all of the colored paper. A few of the people couldn't make the transition to sorting. We created new positions for them. They became responsible for tearing apart telephone books and other materials that were too thick for the shredder. Since the new industrial machine had Tyrannosaurus Rex teeth, it could shred up to 100 pages at a time, which meant that the bulk of the paper went directly on the sorting belt.

The new baler allowed us to sell directly to a paper mill. By eliminating the intermediary recycling center, we received three to five times more per ton of paper. White bales are worth more than mixed bales because there is no need to bleach out the dyes. Mixed paper is worth more than cardboard. The jump in revenue meant that 50 men and women could work at least one shift in the document destruction program every week. Therefore, Green Industries' employees went from living on $44 a month to $250 or $300 for the same time period even if they only worked a day a week.

Did I mention that the industrial shredder could destroy a ton of paper an hour? In addition to having enough income to go out to dinner or a movie, these men and women were saving thousands of trees and conserving gasoline, water and electricity. They are recycling in stark contrast to the city itself. Detroit employs an incinerator to burn all the garbage from 700,000 or 800,000 people each week. The men and women who couldn't read a book or a watch reminded us that everyone is needed on the front line of the green revolution and that liabilities can be assets if we only had eyes to see.

Something That
Doesn't Love a Wall

Twenty years before the Berlin Wall was erected in Germany, a 6-foot-high, 1-foot-thick wall was constructed in northwest Detroit that stretched for half a mile. Its purpose was to serve as a barrier, to keep black people out of a new white housing development. What may surprise you is that the wall wasn't just the result of neighborhood racial prejudice. It was national policy.

The Federal Housing Administration (FHA), founded in 1934, encouraged the segregating practices. Communities with black or Jewish residents were not eligible for federally backed loans. The policy reserved mortgage loans for homogeneous white neighborhoods. The Home Owners Loan Corporation color-coded maps were actually designed to identify neighborhoods with Jewish and black residents. African-American neighborhoods were marked in red, giving us the term "redlining."

Since there was an enclave of African-Americans living in or planning to build houses in the Eight Mile road and Wyoming area, a builder who approached the FHA wanting to develop an all-white subdivision was turned down. He subsequently offered to build the wall to divide the "slum" from his proposed new community, and the FHA reversed its decision.

The Detroit Wailing Wall, as some people refer to it, still stands, running between the backyards of homes from Alfonso Wells Memorial Park to Eight Mile. The only thing different about the 1941 partition today is that its once white concrete is now covered with colorful murals and graffiti-like lettering thanks to Chazz Miller and about 100 other artists. They transformed the shameful wall into a huge canvass that depicts black history in the United States, beginning with Sojourner Truth emerging from the Underground Railroad and including Rosa Parks boarding the bus that is today displayed at Greenfield Village. The artwork doesn't include images from the 1943 or 1967 race riots in Detroit, but the wall's very existence makes it impossible to ignore the history of segregation in the North. The wall is as undeniable as the whites-only swimming pools, bus seats, lunch counters and drinking fountains in the South.

When Cass decided to launch a new Green Industries product line, University of Michigan business professor Bill Lovejoy suggested that we manufacture coaster sets using scenes from the wall. He volunteered his wife, Lois, to take a variety of photographs of the wall artwork to adorn coasters that we would make from glass waste. Then, the business professor mocked up a coaster holder, which was, by his own admission, not up to the quality of the mud mats. In fact, the box looked like a bad Cub Scout project.

Stacy Leigh, the program manager, grew frustrated that she couldn't improve upon Lovejoy's crude holder. She searched the Internet for plans, but even with drawings and assembly directions, her coaster boxes were pathetic. That's when she turned to David. David had worked in the mud mat program the year before, but he struggled mightily with his addiction and ended up in an in-patient rehabilitation program. We didn't see him for several months. When he got out of rehab, he asked if he could come back to work. Since he hadn't done anything wrong on the job, Stacy told him he could return whenever he was ready.

Stacy handed David her Internet plans for a box on his first day back. "Just build this please!" she snarled. An hour and a half later, David reappeared with a gorgeous wooden box. It had rounded corners and a silky smooth sanded surface. Stacy was stunned by David's remarkable aptitude for woodwork.

"Is it OK?" David mistook her silence for disapproval.

She stared at him and started to get a lump in her throat, "Yeah, David. It's more than OK."

Once boxes were figured out, it was time to decide how to finish them. Stacy then asked Marcus to work up some samples using different stains that we already had on hand. He just ran with it. He found all kinds of stains and varnishes on site, and Marcus tried them all. He even started creating his own hues by mixing the colors together. Finally, he came up with three different stains that looked good and would provide customers with light, medium and dark options. But he wasn't done yet. He went on to make the now famous tri-colored version, using all three stains on the same box. Finally, Marcus took a branding iron and added the Cass website to the bottom of the wooden box holders.

Meanwhile, another new hire, Robert, began experimenting with different ways to accelerate the imaging process. It was taking us forever to adhere and trim the photos before sealing them in place and attaching the protective pads. The process Robert developed cut our time in half. It was a good thing, because the Associated Press ran a feature about the wall and our coaster sets. Hundreds of orders came in from all over the United States and even from London, England.

The coaster sets, both simple and stylish, invited customers and others to start otherwise avoidable conversations about race and religion and class. Did you know that there is a Wailing Wall in Detroit? Did you grow up in a neighborhood that was homogeneous? What economic difference has it made to your family to own a house or to inherit one?

The starter conversations sometimes even lead to riskier subjects. What do you know about redlining? What other government policies have benefitted only certain people? The wall stands in a neighborhood that is primarily composed of African-Americans today—who has left the city and why? Did Eight Mile replace the wall as a boundary for race and class? None of the coaster craftsmen own cars. How does the lack of mass transportation limit their access to employment or housing?

Eight to 10 men work in the coaster program. They were all formerly homeless, in addition to being unemployed when they were hired. They skillfully reclaim wood from abandoned houses that have been razed in a city that still has roughly 80,000 structures to demolish. The workers are black and white, young and old, gay and straight, Christian, Muslim and Jewish. They are the anti-wall, symbolically reminding us that prejudice, polarization and systemic discrimination have taken a terrible toll on the region, but that we can decide to make walls a thing of the past. The men challenge us not to make tolerance the goal. Only love can replace hatred or help us surrender privilege.

Detroit Treads

The steady stream of people seeking employment at Cass grew as the economy remained stalled. I had hoped that we could use the treads from the mud mat tires to make sandals to sell. In fact, people were emailing me from everywhere, explaining that they had seen or read about shoes made from rubber in Ethiopia, Kenya, Brazil, Vietnam, Mexico and a score of other places. Why weren't we making them at Cass, they wanted to know?

The answer was simple—steel-belted radials. Prior to the 1970s, cars in the United States used bias ply tires. Since the 1980s, almost all passenger vehicles sold domestically are equipped with radial tires, which have steel cords or steel mesh under the treads. This is good for fuel economy, extending the life of the tires and increasing contact with the road, which improves a car's traction. The problem is that repurposing these tires is a difficult proposition because they are so hard to cut.

I know this because we tried everything shy of a blowtorch—utility knives, handsaws, band saws, skill saws, a Sawzall and even a machete. The blades overheated and broke as fast as we could replace them. The air in the warehouse was dense with smoke and the smell of burnt rubber. What's more, the finished product was crude: unusable rectangles with wires sticking out like Albert Einstein's hair. Then, University of Michigan professors Shaun Jackson and Bill Lovejoy allowed us to engage one of their joint classes for problem solving. At the end of the 2011 fall semester, one of the student groups gave us hope that the sandals could be produced.

The team of five designed a smart-looking sandal and an even better set of branding ideas. Their prototype used the tread rubber to make the sole. They dug out an Old English "D" on the bottom so that wearers would leave a Detroit imprint wherever they went.

Unfortunately, the proposed "D" belonged to the Detroit Tigers.

Even more importantly, the U of M team had identified a company which could remove the steel belt from the tires. One student managed to persuade the company owner to take our treads, remove the metal using a massive shredder with an equally huge magnet and then return the rubber crumb to Cass at no expense! We were in entrepreneurial heaven. The small parts of rubber were then to be mixed with different concentrations of chemicals and fixed into their final sandal state, utilizing molds that the students had prepared. With a little product testing, we could launch the sandals in no time flat.

We asked for the details of their research to set up the work space, only to discover that the chemical in their plan was problematic. To be sure, the undergrads had selected one of the safest binders, but Flexithane still posed some serious health and safety risks. We would have to mitigate the dangers by using protective eyewear and clothing. In the summer months, when it tends to be scorching hot in the warehouse, this could be a challenge.

We would need an eye wash station, too. Everyone would have to be continuously gloved, and just transporting the materials would be very hard. Housekeeping would need to be pristine. Finally, we attended an OSHA seminar in Portland, Oregon, and learned that just traces of the chemical in the air might trigger breathing difficulties. Since some staff members in the warehouse lived with asthma and AIDS, the sandals were scrapped.

I was disappointed and relieved at the same time. A Green Industries' product that required gloves, protective clothing, eye wear, an eyewash station and an expensive ventilation system to propel the toxins outside just didn't jive. There was a disconnect between doing something positive for the environment while wearing the equivalent of a hazmat suit. Cass didn't want to just look green; the agency was committed to sustainable behaviors which would improve the quality of the planet's air, water and land.

A year later, MacGyver, AKA Stephen Schock, came to the rescue. Steve had started his career at General Motors. There he designed the interior of the Corvette. Next, he became a consultant and created farm equipment, including tractors. Finally, our MacGyver took a professorship at Detroit's College for Creative Studies. At the internationally recognized school, Steve Schock is royalty. Just walk with him across campus, and it won't take you long to recognize his popularity. Students swarm him like ants at a picnic. Part of his status comes from the role he plays helping undergrads design sport shoes. Several of his graduates have gone on to work for Nike and Reebok.

We know this quiet, unassuming man as MacGyver because he was able to troubleshoot so many of the sandal problems using just his experience and everyday materials. Steve modified the copyrighted "D" and created molds to mass produce them. He solved the steel extraction dilemma. He researched a lightweight top sole and softer strap materials. Steve gets the credit for finding heat activated glue and for making shoe lasts, forms around which the sandal straps are measured for a proper fit. The day before we launched the flip-flop footwear, Steve coerced his wife, two children and mother into spending hours in the warehouse to help crank the sandals out.

No longer unsophisticated in appearance, Detroit Treads are comfortable, durable and water resistant. They provide good traction in inclement weather, too. Occasionally there are orphan sandals: two different tires are used in making the pair and thus their tread markings are not the same. Still, all of the distinctive summer shoes help Cass reduce our carbon footprint while allowing the customers to "leave their mark."

By the way, in the first month, customers ordered our sandals from 45 different states, generating over $50,000 in sales at $25 a pair. We added a second shift of workers due to the amazing demand.

CHAPTER 6

Getting and Giving

Haunted

Most congregations rely on a set bunch of fundraisers: church dinners, cookbooks and rummage sales. Most of these proven moneymakers haven't been viable options at Cass. Who would come to a rummage sale when the neighborhood is teeming with free stores? Who would buy a church dinner when the area is replete with soup kitchens and food distribution centers? Not many are interested in cookbooks because very few have stoves.

Given our proximity to Wayne State University, once almost entirely a commuter school but increasingly offering residential options, I suggested sponsoring a haunted house. I thought we might be able to attract college volunteers to help construct and staff the house along with college customers to frequent it.

My optimism hit a brick wall at the church board meeting. Lillis Cunningham, a member of Cass Church for more than 40 years, was at the head of the table, dressed in comfortable sweatpants and a blouse covered with a pocketed smock. Her cane rested on the edge of the table, reminding us that her body was riddled with pain. Lillis is a gifted Bible study leader, retired medical lab instructor, one of the few neighborhood homeowners and an overall authority in any manner of secular or sacred subjects. "It doesn't seem very religious," she said.

I wondered why people didn't raise the same objection for rummage sales and spaghetti dinners. Surely the traditional fundraisers don't purport to have spiritual value. I had anticipated a little pushback. "Well," I said, "I thought we could call it the House of Seven Deadly Sins." She was speechless. The whole room went instantly silent. The haunted house was given the green light.

So we used lumber to build 8-foot square panels and then covered them with flame retardant black plastic before attaching them together to make an unsophisticated maze in the church gymnasium. Strategically, we placed fog machines and strobe lights, boom boxes and a wooden bridge with a Plexiglas walkway. A bridge light was activated by motion and revealed the zombie underneath just as the customers stood directly above. It was pretty pathetic that first year.

Still, people came. Teenagers dashed through with their eyes closed and never saw a thing. Some grown men walked behind their girlfriends, holding them at arm's length by the shoulders and using them like shields. All ages of people ran through the thick plastic walls. We started giving workers staple guns so as not to interrupt the traffic while they fastened the coverings back in place. A good number of patrons slipped out of their shoes and refused to re-enter the building to retrieve them. Who would want to go back past the chainsaw-wielding psycho? They dropped their cell phones, their lighters and their glasses, too. The greeter ghoul collected each lost item and held it up outside the front door so that the coward would have to beg for its return in front of those waiting to be admitted.

The second year, we changed the name of the attraction to Detroit Urban Legends, and we added the office spaces in the back hallway. This provided a number of creepy rooms—the door room, the clown room, the mirror room and the white room, which used strobe lights and fog machines to envelop guests, decreasing their visibility to about a foot in front of their faces. Actors dressed in all white would appear out of the smoke and cause the customers to let out bloodcurdling screams. We also beefed up the eerie sound effects, and created a new means of egress through the courtyard.

The back entrance was helpful in dividing up the tiny group of religious demonstrators who appeared the second year. They came wielding placards that warned people about the consequences of worshipping the devil. I don't recall anyone leaving the event as a result of the protests. It's possible that they alerted the media because it wasn't until the second year that reporters started writing stories about the house.

Almost every journalist who requested an interview included a couple of questions about how a church could celebrate a pagan holiday or if it was appropriate for Cass to operate a haunted house. And my response was always the same.

"We are not worshipping the devil. We ask people to use their imaginations. The stuff in the house, none of it is real. The monsters are actors. The blood is food coloring. The sound effects are piped in. Everything is fake, make-believe and intended to be fun. Everyone exits OK, a little scared maybe, but safe.

"We hope that some of the customers will consider situations that are really scary, like being four years old and living in your car with your mother and siblings because you don't have a house. It's terrifying to be in grade school and to worry that your classmates will discover that you're homeless. It's mayhem to stay in a house plagued with domestic violence because you don't know of anywhere to go. That's scary.

"We're raising money to eliminate the terror for homeless women and children. There's a good chance we're raising awareness, as well."

The protestors didn't return for year three.

She's Dead!

The third year of the haunted house, with the help of two mischievous skilled trades volunteers from the Ford Livonia Transmission Plant, we added the basement level of the church as part of the attraction. The word 'basement' sounds so innocent. The church basement dates back to the 19th century. It included a room affectionately called the dungeon, due to its dirt floor and stone walls. In the dungeon, the sewer system was partially exposed, the lighting was minimal and the sounds and smells from the steam boiler next door belonged in a Stephen King novel. The best feature of the basement space was that fake rats weren't required.

There are no windows downstairs, so it was pitch black in the basement at night. We eliminated the music there because we wanted people to hear the pandemonium of others screaming in the gym area directly above them. They heard the drop windows slamming, the tilt floor banging and people racing to get through the maze, too. Every night a few people refused to go down the back stairwell to the basement. They were forced to retrace their steps out of the house. None seemed overly concerned about our no-refund policy at that point.

Thirty to 35 menacing volunteers were needed to adequately staff the attraction each night. We checked their criminal backgrounds and offered a minimum amount of scare training in advance. Unbeknownst to the customers, each evening about half of the actors were afraid to be in the house, so we placed them in the cavity between the walls. There they unleashed terror by moving items, making sinister noises and manipulating electric switches.

The brave actors put on costumes and masks or make-up. They moved within the maze and its many rooms to shock folks as they jumped out of things—a coffin, a sofa, a refrigerator, a dog house, a jail cell. At one point, our customers walked through a morgue where corpses hung down in body bags, and the actors just stood still until the frightened guests bumped into them. Here the visitors generally swore. Some wet themselves. The key to it all was to lull people into a fake sense of security and then surprise them whenever possible.

All of the volunteer workers were at least 16 years of age. The reasoning was that every once in a while, the visitors become so frightened that they hauled off and punched a performer. Violence wasn't their aim. They just lost control momentarily because they were jolted, like others who were so panicked that they fell to the floor. At any rate, we maintained the minimum age requirement so that a child actor wouldn't get hurt.

On Halloween night, I had just let a new group into the house when Rick ran up to me between the walls. Rick was tall for 17 and had gotten into trouble earlier that night for asking attractive girls for their phone numbers in the white room instead of scaring them. Beyond that, he had always been a bit of a prankster.

"Rev. Fowler," he said, trying to catch his breath, "someone's dead."

"Cut it out Rick," I responded. "That's not funny."

"No, Rev. Fowler," he reacted, "she's dead in the back hallway."

"What are you talking about?" I knew that we had a problem from the tone of his voice.

"Everyone out of the house!" I yelled as I turned on the gym lights and summoned one of the two nurses who were volunteering. We sprinted to the back hall, where I saw the customer lying flat on the naked tile floor. All the color was gone from her face, and she was unresponsive. I couldn't tell if she was even breathing. Our nurse started asking the actors questions and I called 911.

By the time the ambulance arrived, we had learned that our young patron had had a seizure. Evidently she was epileptic and didn't know it. The strobe lights had undoubtedly triggered her reaction. Fortunately she came with friends, so we were able to contact her parents. The paramedics checked her vital signs, asked her for some basic information, and then loaded her onto a stretcher to take her to a nearby hospital. They rolled her out the Selden Street door and inserted her into the back of the ambulance.

The customers waiting in line watched everything, but they knew nothing. We were supposed to close at 11 p.m. that night, but the line kept growing until it stretched three quarters of the way down the block. People kept coming until 2 a.m. We were delighted that our young customer recovered, and overwhelmed by the unexpected sales. It certainly has crossed our minds to stage a medical emergency in the future.

Location, Location, Location

Word spread about our twisted haunted house and people started arriving in droves from distant places. They couldn't get enough of the animated props and creepy actors. As sales climbed, we became obsessed with adding new effects. Several of our volunteers visited area haunts, and a few even traveled to other states to borrow best practices. Life-sized mannequins were purchased and strategically placed in the maze. A guillotine was installed. A motion-sensor-activated train horn and light went in.

Despite all these excellent embellishments, I really just wanted to rent space for the haunted house at the Art Center Music School, one block north of the church on Cass Avenue.

Prior to being occupied by the music school, the building and its art deco addition belonged to the William R. Hamilton Funeral Home. It would have been a perfect setting with its creaky wood floors and mortuary layout. Even more significant, Erich Weiss had been embalmed at Hamilton.

Fresh from Montreal, Weiss was no stranger to Detroit. He was a regular visitor. This last time he spent the evening at the Garrick Theater across the street from the Book Cadillac Hotel, but he became sick and collapsed at the end of the show. Weiss was rushed to Grace Hospital and the medical staff removed his ruptured appendix during emergency surgery.

However, it was too late, and Erich Weiss, AKA Harry Houdini, died at 1:26 p.m. on Halloween, October 31, 1926. There is disagreement about the cause of his death, but no one questions that Houdini's body was taken to the Hamilton Funeral Home. His corpse was embalmed on the second floor and placed, temporarily, in a new casket that he had planned to use in future performances. The former funeral home would be the perfect place for a haunted house, especially since the magician dabbled in communicating with the dead. I just couldn't get the music school board of directors to understand why our event was more important than offering music lessons to the neighborhood children.

We were able to score a couple of caskets, one of those lamps that stand next to the casket so you can really look at the dead person's make-up, a lectern, folding chairs, a cemetery sign and a stuffed pheasant from a defunct funeral home. Geoff Sleeman, a former Cass board member and the Facilities Director at the College for Creative Studies, called to say that they had acquired and were renovating a building on Ferry Street that had once belonged to Mr. James Fritz. Jimmy Fritz was a funeral director in Detroit for nearly 70 years. His 2012 obituary pointed out that he was in charge of the arrangements and burial for former Mayor Coleman A. Young. (Fritz stood watch for the entire time that Young's body was in repose at the Charles A. Wright Museum of African-American History.) We, of course, were honored to take possession of his funeral home items.

The other exciting acquisition was a used hearse. It had a sleek, slightly rusted white body with stiff curtains that concealed the spider web covered windows. We got it cheap since it didn't have an engine. The local garage towed it to the church and we mounted one of those rotating flashing lights on the top of it to draw the attention of people driving by. When it wasn't in use in October, the hearse was stored at the back of the Scott parking lot. Frequently youth groups would pose beside the hearse for pictures.

Late one September, the tow truck arrived, hitched up the hearse with chains and began hauling it south on the Lodge Freeway. The driver checked his rear view mirror to make sure everything was as it should be when he saw 25 to 30 rats jumping out of the hearse and dashing in every conceivable direction in their attempts not to be flattened by the cars traveling 60 miles an hour behind the tow truck. The cars were swerving frantically to avoid the cat-sized rodents. Can't you just hear the dinner conversation? "Really, honey, I was driving on the expressway next to this hearse that was being towed by a truck when huge rats started soaring through the air like the flying monkeys in the *Wizard of Oz.*"

We were making $10,000 a season for our work with women and children in need of support. And at the same time the haunted house was increasing awareness about the growing number of homeless women and children. (From 2007 to 2009, the percentage of homeless children had skyrocketed by 22 percent in Michigan.)

Then, someone decided that the Cass haunted house needed a city permit. At that time, it seemed like it would have been easier to break the sound barrier than to obtain a permit from the city. During a five-year period, we completed the same notarized paperwork every fall, paid a few thousand dollars in inspection fees, and walked health and safety and fire department officials through our building nine different times. We provided evidence of egress maps, no smoking signs, fire retardant sprays, smoke detectors, and trained firewatchers. We submitted legal statements promising to limit the number of people admitted into the house at one time (haunters understand that small groups are easiest to scare anyway).

The city closed the basement permanently one year because we didn't have a fire suppression system, and then the city shut down the house for three different nights the following year. Rather than continuing to haggle over changing permit rules and inspections, we moved our haunting outside in 2013. We took over the acres between the Scott Building and Mom's

Place. The property was Bates Motel scary with just the light of the moon. The uneven ground thwarted everyone's equilibrium, while the sway of the trees in the wind caused their hair to stand on end. It was a little cold, and rain was no fun, but no permit was required.

We had to forego our haunted house slogan: "Cass Church, we'll scare the hell out of you." The new location gave the attraction a new name though. The haunt is just off the Lodge Freeway. You exit at Elmhurst and so, instead of Detroit Urban Legends, we now operate Nightmare on Elmhurst.

Prospective Donor

A prospective donor visited my office one day. She was a nicely dressed, middle-aged white woman in sensible shoes. We had never met before, but somehow she had heard of Cass and came to see things for herself.

She sat down and proceeded to grill me to determine if our organization was worthy of her support. She seemed content with my responses until I mentioned that Cass operates a free medical clinic. She interrupted me mid-sentence asking, "And what about contraceptives?" Her question felt like an ambush. Here we go again, I thought to myself.

"If you are asking me if I am pro-life," I responded. "I am. I believe that life is sacred."

"Good." She opened her checkbook on the corner of my desk and began writing.

Although I had passed her litmus test, I was far from finished. "I am pro-life before a child is born, and I am pro-life when a baby is a baby. I am pro-life if you are talking about prenatal care, child abuse or Head Start."

She stopped writing.

"I've got to tell you," I continued. "I'm pro-life when it comes to allocating funds for public education and when we are deciding issues of juvenile justice and lifetime sentences. Yep, I'm pro-life."

It didn't matter what I was saying anymore. She wasn't even looking at me. The woman stood up as if doing so would get me to shut up. But I didn't.

"I'm pro-life when it comes to universal health care, climate change, cigarette smoking, domestic abuse and war." I wondered if she had noticed the "Who Would Jesus Bomb?" bumper sticker on the book shelf behind me.

She started making big, slow strides toward the door, like the astronauts did when they walked on the moon. "I'm pro-life if someone is suicidal or if a person is on death row," I said because I was on a roll.

She slammed the door behind her. No check was exchanged.

So I continued, now talking to myself, "I am pro-life, and so we distribute condoms to adults who have reached the conclusion that they are not prepared to be parents, and given the opportunity, I'd do the same in a New York minute elsewhere to stop millions of people from contracting HIV or children from being orphaned by AIDS."

The Poor Will Always Be With You

When I teach a public relations course at the University of Michigan-Dearborn in the summer, I like to make the point that how you say something is just as important as what you are trying to communicate. I use an example from a crisis-intervention training seminar I attended years ago. You write a simple sentence on the board or project it on a screen. It states: "I never said you were stupid."

"Does anyone know what that means?" I ask. All of the students look up from their cell phones and laptops. Most nod their heads affirmatively.

"Can someone tell me how you interpret it?" A student will say that the statement means that the speaker denies having said that another person is stupid.

Then, I purposely accent a different word using a pointer each time I repeat the sentence.

"**I** never said you were stupid. What does that mean?" I ask. The class answers in surround sound, "Someone else did."

"I **never** said you were stupid." Hands shoot up. "It means I would never do that."

"OK," I continue, "I never **said** you were stupid." A couple pupils announce, "I thought it though."

I re-read the sentence. "I never said **you** were stupid." The class has caught on. "I said someone else was stupid," a normally quiet student responds.

Again, "I never said you **were** stupid." "You are stupid!" comes the chorus.

Finally, I read, "I never said you were **stupid**." No student is left behind. Each calls out a different something else that the person said rather than "stupid."

"That's paraverbal communication," I tell them. "It means that the same words can have entirely different meanings. Just change your tone or volume or cadence and the meaning is altered. Stress a different word and the sentence is not the same."

Sometimes, a student is unconvinced by the illustration, so I am forced to give a real-life example. "Do you know the words to 'Happy Birthday'?" Of course, they respond. "Sing it to me," I say. The class does as instructed. Then I push a little more, "What does the song mean?" Everyone agrees that the song conveys well wishes on the anniversary of someone's birth.

"You are right," I say dimming the classroom lights. Compliments of YouTube, I start the video clip of Marilyn Monroe singing "Happy Birthday" to JFK in a very sexy voice and a skin-tight dress in front of 15,000 spectators at Madison Square Garden for the president's 45th birthday. "Never forget that how you say something can be as important as what you say."

Speaking in church settings, I sometimes do that same exercise with an often quoted text, "The poor will always be with you." The vast majority of people place the accent on "always," indicating there is nothing you can do to eliminate poverty. There will always be poor people. Jesus said so in red letters, so don't waste your time. Then, I quote Jim Wallis, who puts the emphasis on "with you," meaning if there are poor people, you need to be with them. Then we inevitably talk about where poor people congregate.

If you aren't sure where to find a few poor people, just ask to speak with the "direct care" employees at any small to mid-sized nonprofit. Like so many citizens in our country, these folks work full time, some even work two full-time jobs, but they are generally paid poorly. They are the working poor.

When I arrived at Cass, staff wages were low and stagnant. A few employees hadn't had a raise in six years. This is not an indictment of the previous administration. A huge problem for not-for-profits is that many are heavily reliant on government grants. These awards tend to be locked at the award level indefinitely. So, for instance, even with a generous award, if the dollar amount remains the same for several years or a decade, something has to give. Insurance, health insurance, gasoline, food, utilities and the other costs all regularly increase. Since your grant amounts do not grow, staff compensation tends to lag behind.

With the exception of 2008, we have been able to scrape together annual merit raises for 20 years. What's more, the entry-level staff members and direct care employees earn a couple of dollars more than the minimum wage. Our goal, of course, is to pay a living wage. Cass employees work long, hard hours, taking risks and making sacrifices to work with poor people. We don't want them to finish a shift and worry about feeding their families, making their car payment or mailing their mortgage payment. We don't want them to forego medical treatment or filling medication prescriptions because they lack the funds. We certainly don't want them retiring only to join the ranks of people needing our services.

At first, with no pension plan in place, we decided to give every staff member a $100 savings bond at the annual holiday staff party (a few of our employees are Jewish and a couple are Muslim). It wasn't much, but we hoped that they would stash it away. We thought it would give them a small start for the future. The majority of the employees waited the required six months, and then cashed the bonds in without any interest.

After three years of the bonds, we established a SEP plan at Cass. This retirement benefit allowed us to pick a salary percentage for all the staff members. Although, for example, two percent meant a greater amount for executive staff members than entry-level workers, each employee would have something in a retirement account. Each person decided how the money was invested. Unfortunately, once after the waiting period was over, nearly all of the lowest paid people withdrew their funds, minus a hefty penalty.

The fact that Cass employees didn't have a cushion for an emergency or savings for retirement really troubled me. Our people were living from paycheck to paycheck. Over half the staff wasn't participating in the health insurance plan because it required a copay. Folks were forced to juggle bills when beset with emergency needs. Some workers relied on cash advances and other predatory lending practices. Tow trucks hauled cars off our parking lot for payment failure. I watched garnishment notices arrive weekly.

Abandoning the SEP plan, we tried 403 B accounts, which are the nonprofit equivalent of the 401 K. There were fewer than 10 takers.

At the same time, I noticed that some of the staff members were spending incredible sums of money gambling. A few were playing as much as five or 10 dollars a day on the lottery. Others waited until payday and then rushed down to one of Detroit's three casinos. They all said the same thing, "If I hit big, Rev. Fowler, I'll give some money to Cass." I wasn't holding my breath.

I used every opportunity to expound on the impossible odds of getting rich by gambling. Then, I caved … If you can't beat 'em, join 'em.

"What are your chances of winning the Mega Millions?" I asked at an all-agency in-service. They knew that it was a long shot. "Would you be happy if I could give you better odds? What if I said your chances were one in a hundred? One in 50? One in 10?"

The whole room looked at me like I was speaking Russian. I pulled a note card out of my briefcase and read the six names of the non-executives who were participating in Cass' 403 B plan. I had someone shuffle the cards and drop them into a hat. Another employee drew a card. I read the name from the card out loud and asked her to come forward. Then, I presented the surprised staff member a crisp $100 bill.

"You like to bet?" I said. "Good. Put at least $5-a-paycheck into a 403 B plan, and your name will go into the hat. Every month we will draw a new name and the winner will get $100 cash. If every staff member enrolls, your odds will be 1 in 100. If fewer sign up, your odds improve. Even if we never draw your name, you will not have lost a penny and you will have money in a retirement account. Over time it will grow. Your money will work for you. If your name does comes up, you'll have $100 to spend any way you want."

Today, almost half of the hundred employees contribute to the payroll deduction retirement plan. Most make small contributions, but participants have begun to appreciate the concept of compounding. We have a goal of fostering long-term retirement planning by providing an agency match for employee contributions, but, until that is possible, the "gambling" incentive has dealt a small blow to economic vulnerability.

Another staff investment that has demonstrated a good return has been the tuition reimbursement program. All full-time and part-time staff members are eligible for the funding if they're enrolled in college or graduate courses. Their degree does not have to coincide with their job responsibilities at Cass. We have encouraged and helped six people get their associate's degree, eight have earned a bachelor's, and three have obtained a master's degree in the last 15 years. More are in process, including one director who is working on a PhD.

Two small asset-building programs for CCSS employees have been worthy of note. The agency has sold donated cars to residents and staff members needing transportation. The staff members can make the payments through payroll deduction. The vehicles are sold "as is," so we recommend that the buyers have a mechanic inspect the car first. After showing proof of insurance and affixing a license plate, the new owners are on their way. A car makes upward mobility possible for countless people.

The same type of transaction is used with donated houses. I'll never forget the day an 84-year- old woman handed her house keys to a 22-year-old staff member. The senior could no longer manage the house, and she was moving into a retirement community. The young woman donated $5,000 to Cass using a no-interest, small payment installment arrangement, and she became a debt-free homeowner in less than two years. It was a life-affirming exchange. I still have the picture the young woman texted me. She was beaming in the front hallway of her house, holding up her keys.

Finally, next to no one had life insurance at Cass until Ken Norton died in 1998. Ken Norton worked at East Side Ministries. One day he was held up at gunpoint in the office there; the next day he was back to work because he knew that the men and women would be worried about him. He was a large man with an infectious laugh, who battled with diabetes and heart disease. Just 40 when he passed away, Ken had a heart attack. He left behind two young daughters, but no life insurance.

Poor people are doubly burdened when a loved one dies. Like the rest of us, they experience consuming grief, but they also must simultaneously raise the money to lay the deceased to rest. Often this means choosing cremation because it is significantly cheaper than a burial. Yet, even with cremation, a family must solicit around $2,000. Absolutely nothing will happen until the dollars are raised. Family members, neighbors, co-workers and church members are asked to contribute for the burial services. If it requires a couple of weeks or months to secure the money, that's how long the funeral will be delayed. We paid to bury Ken in 1998; then, the agency purchased a life insurance policy to cover employees.

Our mantra is "Fighting Poverty. Creating Opportunity." We interpret it to mean that poverty can be eradicated and that opportunities must be cultivated for all people. Working at Cass shouldn't make people poor. Just as it is important to donors that our administrative costs are minimal, and to the IRS that the agency avoids conflicts of interest, it is imperative for us to stress decent incomes and adequate benefits. Without this emphasis, our words lack authority to address domestic or global poverty. Speaking to subjects like the millennial development goals or socially responsible investing would be meaningless, if the Cass slogan didn't apply to our own employees.

Hot Water

Getting from the parking lot to my office can take forever. People stop me with every imaginable request—bus tickets, baptisms, cigarettes, rides. There is always an introduction to an auditor, a new employee, a volunteer, a donor and even protective services. One afternoon, returning from God knows where, I was approached by a man from the community. "Rev. Fowler," he stationed himself in my path, "can I have some water?"

"Sure," I said, walking around him.

"Can I have some hot water?" he went on.

"OK," I answered, mulling over why he thought the temperature of the water would change my response.

"You don't understand, do you?" he kept at it. In fact, I was clueless.

"No," I admitted.

"Well, I have a job, but they cut my hours. I haven't been able to keep up with my bills. I don't have any hot water," he said.

"A friend of mine told me about these bags. They're like those pizza containers that keep the food warm. Well, anyway, I bought one and I thought if I could come here and fill it up with hot water, I could rush home and take a shower," he said, demonstrating by making a fist above his head and opening it as if to release the water from a thermal pouch.

Mortified, I thought to myself, what kind of country do we live in when a man with a job has to bathe this way? "Yeah," I said, "you can use our hot water."

A day or two later, I noticed that someone had slipped a white envelope under my door. It was unmarked and contained three dollars. The next day an envelope was there again. The third and fourth day, the pattern continued. Every day, like manna in the wilderness, it was just supplied. Sometimes the envelope held change, but always it added up to three dollars.

Finally, I realized that it was our neighbor. He was leaving the contribution every time he returned for shower water.

When I ran into him in the hall next, I stopped him and quietly whispered in his ear, "You know we don't need your money."

"It's not about you," he said.

An O. Henry Christmas

The gifts of the Magi make perfect sense theologically, but the presents certainly weren't practical. The arrival of a child requires diapers and bottles, cribs and strollers, feeding supplies and bathing equipment. Try taking frankincense or myrrh to your next baby shower. The mother-to-be might appreciate the gold. As with Mary and Joseph, she could sell it to pay for a trip to Egypt or Hawaii, but surely with a baby on the way, other items will be needed sooner rather than later.

Sometimes gifts at Cass resemble those of the traveling kings in terms of their usefulness. One Christmas Eve stands out in my memory. Volunteers were serving a hot dinner prior to the candlelight service. Some people had come for the meal and worship, others just stopped in to dine. Either way, as each guest finished eating, a volunteer would give the person a nicely wrapped present. The items were simple things like fancy hand lotion or a warm scarf. People were generally pleased to receive something.

Then, from the far end of the gym, I heard a woman scream, "Wind chimes! What the 'f--k' do I need wind chimes for, I'm homeless!" Needless to say, the volunteer was speechless. I hot-stepped it over to the site and attempted to help them resolve the issue thinking all the while that although the guest had a colorful vocabulary, she had a point. What do you do with wind chimes when you don't have a porch?

Carol Shissler, who had been in charge of the senior programs at Cass for over a decade, recognized an ocean of unmet needs and established an "adoption" system for the holidays. In short, individuals and parents compiled lists of what they wanted for Christmas, including clothing sizes. Then, generous donors would take the lists to area stores and buy items for those who needed help.

One of the problems with the system was that some recipients had exhaustive and expensive lists and some barely asked for anything. Another problem was that several donors were able to provide many posh presents while others, although equally bighearted, were only able to give one or two small things.

Both problems revealed themselves on D-day—distribution day. Recipient parents, many with children in tow, would sit in the lunchroom waiting for their name to be called off. One by one, they would come forward to receive the things that were brought in for them by donors. The gifts arrived at Cass wrapped and unwrapped, in huge garbage bags and in small brown lunch-sized sacks. One family would need to make multiple trips to take away computer games, a big- screen television and a portable basketball set-up while another followed with just a package of underwear and a book. Maybe this is exactly what they had requested, maybe not.

Needless to say, despite the Christmas carols playing on a cassette player and the homemade cookies and punch available, by the middle of the give-away, the mood of the room was mixed. Some folks were elated. Others felt slighted. Tempers occasionally flared. Fights ensued. For all the good intentions, there was no "peace on earth, goodwill toward people." It was D-day at Cass.

At the conclusion of one particular D-day, shortly after we moved into the Scott Building, I received a phone call from a man named Steve. "I'm going to buy a new bike for Victor, OK?"

"I'm sorry, how do you know Victor?" Victor was a 6-year-old in our 90-day Family Shelter who could have been featured in a commercial for Ritalin.

"I was dropping off gifts today and I met him on the front steps."

Are you sure you don't want to buy him a car, I thought to myself. "Well, you may want to reconsider," I said. "If Victor gets a bike and his siblings don't, what will his brothers and sister think? If he is the only child in the shelter, which has 24 children, to receive a bike, how will the rest react? What if his mother doesn't want him to have a bike yet? Where will he keep the bike? He, of course, will need a helmet and durable lock. Are you sure he knows how to ride a bike? … "

"I hadn't thought about that," he said. "Are you saying I can't give him a bike?"

"No," I replied. "I'm saying it may not be the best gift for him at this time."

We talked for a while more and I made several suggestions that would allow Steve to be generous and allow Victor's mother to be involved in the present selecting process, but by the time I hung up, it was clear to me that we needed a new way to exchange gifts for Christmas.

"Here's what I want to try," I told board member Amy Bouque. "A Christmas store. We'll give donors a list of suggested presents for a variety of ages and both genders. Then, we'll arrange the items in the church gym as if it were a department store—there will be a section for clothing, another one for games and toys and a third area will have books. Pre-approved parents will pay a dollar per child so that there is the dignity of purchasing the gifts. Then, they will walk through the store picking out several gifts for each of their children. We can even scrounge up some shopping carts for the day. At the end, volunteers can either help them wrap their purchases or give them paper, tape, ribbon and name cards so the parents can do it at home."

Although Amy hadn't been involved in the Christmas program, she was a human resources executive with a huge heart and a brilliant mind. Amy voiced some skepticism. Indeed, there were real risks involved. The donors really liked shopping for their adopted families.

"You see, here's the thing Amy. The way we are doing it now has robbed the mothers and fathers of the shopping experience. You remember Jim and Della in O. Henry's *The Gift of the Magi* story? The couple was dirt poor, but still each wanted to give the other something meaningful. Each scrimped and saved and sacrificed with joy. In this new system, our donors can gift the parents the gladness that comes with selecting and giving presents."

Would people donate to the store instead of to families? Time alone would tell. We started collecting items right after Halloween. They were kept under lock and key at the Scott Building so that no one would be tempted to steal anything. On a cold December Sunday after church services, a throng of volunteers arrived to set up the store for Monday. I asked Karen to drive up to Scott to organize the volunteers who had gone directly there. She complied while I welcomed the onsite people who began setting up tables and hanging signs.

Karen stood in about 6 inches of snow in front of the Scott Building, dressed in her Sunday best, including hose and high heel shoes. She waited next to the moving truck as the helpers brought out hundreds of boxes and bags stuffed with treasures. "What are you doing out here dressed like that?" Amy asked Karen.

"I got Faithed," she answered.

"What?" Amy was confused.

"Faith cornered me after church and I couldn't come up with an excuse!" They both laughed. A month later, Amy had some "gotFaith?" t-shirts made in the vein of the more famous "gotMilk?" I found it slightly offensive, but we've sold several thousand of the t-shirts since then in every imaginable color combination.

Not only did the donors exceed our expectations with the quantity and quality of gifts, but many volunteers were eager to staff the store. They stocked the shelves, helped parents look for sizes, handled food and beverages for the shoppers, and stood in for Santa's elves as gift wrappers.

Highly organized and the consummate problem-solver, Amy said, "Since we have extra people, why don't we assign each parent a personal shopper."

"I don't think that's a good idea," I told her.

"Why not?" she wondered.

"You have to remember that African-Americans routinely get followed through stores as if they are going to steal something. They might interpret the shadowing personal shoppers as suspicious counter clerks or security guards watching their every move."

"I never would have thought of that," she admitted.

The Christmas store dramatically changed the mood of gift giving at Cass. The parents were grateful. The volunteers enjoyed the exchanges. Most of the donors understood the reasons for the store, and their support was evidenced by the avalanche of games, toys, dolls, and clothing we received. Occasionally someone would say that they really preferred the adopt-a-family model, and a few more moved on to other agencies, especially those that allowed them to deliver the gifts right to the children themselves.

Still, a couple of incidents from the Cass store confirmed that the swap was the right thing to do. Each year, a gentleman and his wife provided a hefty check to pay for 300 new coats. Everything in the store is new. All year long, we are happy to pass out used things, but not for Christmas. Anyway, the coats, in all of their bright colors, were hung by size on coat racks made by one of our volunteers. They fill an entire wall. Parents are allowed to take a coat for every child that needs one. It's a humbling experience to watch the women and men deliberate for long periods of time as they select jackets for their children.

One woman came into the coat section and announced to the volunteer that she had taken a coat the previous year that didn't fit her child. "I'm sorry," the volunteer offered. Then, the shopper pulled the coat out of a black garbage bag. It was protected still in its clear plastic store wrapper.

"I wanted to bring it back just the way I got it. Some other little girl needs a brand new coat," she said, not realizing that the volunteer would be moved to tears.

Every Christmas Eve, after worship, I deliver a stocking to every resident in each Cass building or shelter. Margaret Valade's Bible study group from Birmingham makes all of the stockings and packs them with snack foods and trinkets that are age- and gender-specific. It was about 11 o'clock and I was almost done with my Santa duties when I stopped at our facility for homeless women and children with AIDS. There, as I went door to door dropping off the loot, at least four of the mothers invited me in, not just to see their trees, but the presents beneath them. They told me about every gift and solicited my feedback about their choices. I knew then and there that in the morning, the parents would be as elated as their children because we had allowed them to give meaningful gifts, like O. Henry's wise men.

CHAPTER 7

The D

Andy and the Rental

Andy's dad was a pastor in Roscommon, Michigan. Rev. Ken Christler "planted" the church near Higgins Lake, and as beautiful as the area is, he felt that Andy should be exposed to other places and people. So, he sent his son down to Cass. First, it was to volunteer for a day. Then, he came for a weekend. When Ken was transferred to pastor a church in Alpena, five hours north of Detroit and two hours from an expressway, Ken decided that Andy should spend a couple of months in the city.

It was the summer before Andy's senior year in high school. Ken and his wife, Bonnie, drove Andy on the five hour trip down to Detroit. Since I had a meeting that night, the trio stopped at Cass Church to say hello to me and to pick up my house keys and the alarm code. Then they dropped Andy off at my house. Ken helped Andy unload his luggage from the trunk, but Bonnie never moved from the passenger's seat. Andy walked over to his mother's window after his bags were safely on the curb. She nervously rolled the glass down about an inch, put her mouth up to the small crack and said, "I love you. Be good." And then his parents were gone.

There are a number of great neighborhoods in Detroit, like Boston Edison, Indian Village, Palmer Woods and Rosedale Park. My rental house was in one of them. Woodbridge is a stone's throw from Wayne State University and about a mile from Cass Church. The house had two stories with four bedrooms, two bathrooms and a small yard with a deck. What's more, the landlord had painted the house loud shades of blue and gold, so you never had to provide detailed directions for guests.

Andy made his way up the steps. He unlocked and opened the iron security screen door before doing the same with the heavy wooden door. Once inside, he put down his bags and typed the code into the keypad below the light switch. Then he walked into the living room in the hopes of watching a movie or grabbing a nap when the alarm suddenly went off at a deafening volume. My dog Ziggy, woke up, jumped down from the sofa and stared at the houseguest as if to say: *Can't you turn that thing off? I'm trying to sleep.* Andy tried. He frantically typed the code in again and again with no results. It screamed for almost 10 minutes.

When the alarm system shut itself off, Andy thought it was safe to move once more. He was wrong. He started toward the bathroom and the thunderous alarm resumed. It wasn't until that moment that he saw the motion detector laser beams dissecting the room. He dropped to the floor and remained there, immobile, until the sound stopped.

After almost 90 minutes alone in the house with the dog, my new unpaid intern had lost all hope of a rescue when he heard a car door close. Thank you Jesus, there was a knock on the door. Andy stood up and accidently activated the siren once more as he raced to get to the front of the house. He thought his prayers had been answered when he saw a large, African-American cop standing at the security door.

Andy began blurting out his entire life story at breakneck speed, ending with everything that had happened that day. The officer said just four words, "Is that a dog?"

Again, Andy rambled on about being from Alpena and having a father who was a pastor, but the officer had ceased concentrating on his words. Officer Braveheart was fixated on my elderly, slightly deaf and increasingly balding dog—the one standing mute behind the blabbering teen. The policeman told Andy to call the alarm company and explain what had happened. Then he left without even asking Andy his name.

Following directions, Andy searched the keypad for the company's contact information. There was an 800 number listed in fine print. Unfortunately, the cordless phone was on the other side of the room. He stood frozen for a few minutes, knowing that the alarm would sound if he moved. When Ziggy returned to the sofa for some more shut-eye without tripping the alarm, Andy realized that if he could stay lower than the dog, he could move about freely.

Crawling army-style, he traveled awkwardly across the floor to stay under the lasers. He wiggled and jerked like he was in a 007 spy movie. The dog, of course, just stared at him. Andy finally grabbed the phone off its cradle and slithered back to the door, his stomach never leaving the blue carpeting. He dialed the telephone number listed on the keypad and an electronic voice gave him prompts.

Enter your phone number, etc. Then the voice issued a strange command. "If you are a man, press 1. If you are a woman, press 2." He pressed one without thinking. Next the voice asked him for a credit card. Andy decided that he had made a mistake because he was answering for himself, but he was staying with a woman. He hung up the phone and tried again, this time answering as a woman.

Andy kept running into dead ends. He re-dialed four or five times. Finally, when the voice asked for a credit card, since the soon to be twelfth grader didn't have one, he just listened. "The price of the call will be $1.99 per minute," the voice said. The telephone number on the keypad was wrong, undoubtedly out of date. Andy had repeatedly been calling a telephone sex-chat line.

Out of options, Andy ignored the alarm. If he needed something, he became a snake. He crawled commando style to the kitchen for a glass of water. He crept on his hands and knees to the bathroom. Ziggy continued to watch Andy, but she wouldn't sit with him. She must have concluded that there was something not quite right with the boy. Four hours later, I came home from my meeting. Andy was curled up under the alarm keypad next to his unopened luggage, asleep in the fetal position. The dog was watching television from the couch in the other room.

In case you are thinking that the experience ruined Andy for life, he continued to return to Cass summer after summer. He earned a bachelor's degree from Central Michigan University, and then a master's from Wayne State. Today, he is a speech pathologist, living in a major city. And his mom, Bonnie, comes to Cass regularly on her own.

This Old House

There are times when what you think is just dead wrong.

As when I started my seminary internship at Walpole Prison (now called Cedar Junction because the town of Walpole, Massachusetts, allegedly no longer wanted to be associated with the penitentiary—which just seemed wrong and caused me to sing the Petticoat Junction theme song). I walked into the maximum security prison expecting to meet callous inmates who resembled Hannibal Lecter. But they didn't. The men were young and mostly reminded me of the college students I knew back in Michigan.

I was equally stunned when I started at Cass. A couple of pastors whom I both liked and respected talked to me about my housing at Cass Church. In the Methodist appointment system, ministers live in the parsonage, a church-owned house used by the pastor or parson. Since Cass Church didn't own a house, the previous pastor had been given a housing allowance, which he used to buy a house. It was the same arrangement the senior pastor before him had had.

My colleagues surprised me when they said that I couldn't buy a house. I needed to rent a house. The two actually flabbergasted me when they went on to indicate that I was expected to rent the home that the former senior pastor had purchased. His new church owned a parsonage where he would reside, so the house he had bought for himself would have to be rented or sold.

"Let me see if I understand this right." I thought maybe I was losing my mind. "You are telling me to rent Rev. So-and-So's parsonage?"

"That's right," my friend answered.

There was nothing wrong with the former pastor's house. It was in fine condition and located in a lovely neighborhood just across Woodward Avenue from Palmer Park, one of the finest sections of the city.

Weighing my words to the extent possible while I was seething with anger, I said, "So, for 40 years it was OK for the Cass pastor to buy a home, but now it's not and you want me to pay the former pastor to live in his house?"

"That's right," he answered again, as if he was glad that I reached the correct conclusion.

Then he added, "You know, Rev. So-and-So has a mortgage and a family."

"Well that makes sense," I concurred, "or at least it would have in 1884. But this is 1984. I'm not paying off his mortgage. If I have to rent, I'll find someplace closer to the church."

Did I wax on about how the church staff would be cut from three pastors to two upon my arrival and thus my workload would be significantly more? Or about how my starting salary would be substantially less than the man with the mortgage? No, I was unmoored by the situation. I let my Gloria Steinem moment slip away.

For six years I rented a house about a mile from the church, using my housing allowance. Then the Detroit Annual Conference of the United Methodist Church changed its policy so that any clergy person could purchase property. I started immediately looking for a home. The Cass Corridor (as it was called back then) was almost exclusively apartments, so I started searching in Woodbridge, Brush Park and Corktown for someplace with a yard for the dog. I needed a mortgage that was affordable, and I wanted a place that was a walkable and bikeable distance to the church.

It was love at first sight. I stopped my car in the middle of the street because I couldn't believe that there was a For Sale sign in front of the old Victorian. A historic marker next to the front bay window explained that the two-story house was built by Prussian carpenter Joseph Esterling in 1864 while Abraham Lincoln was president and the Civil War was raging. Esterlings occupied the dwelling for its first 100 years.

Evidence of Esterling's craftsmanship was everywhere—the small eaves brackets, rounded window panels, elongated columns on the tiny front porch. Above the imposing wood front doors, the building's original address was displayed in stained glass. A different address was mounted next to one of the pillars (thus confusing pizza-delivery people, who are generally unaware that the city's address system changed in the early 1920s). Because I'd been living for six years without a designated parking space, the house's driveway also appealed to me. I decided that the off-street parking would compensate for having a crawl space instead of a basement.

It would take me a week to coordinate a tour of the interior. I walked through, smitten with every historic feature: 10-foot-tall ceilings, stenciling on the painted walls and period wallpaper elsewhere. Wainscoting accented a few rooms. There were thick hardwood floorboards in the entrance hall and a cherry banister along the staircase, a wood-burning stove in the family room and a claw-foot tub in an oversized bathroom. Obviously, indoor plumbing belonged to the more recent addition. Just 27 feet wide at its thickest and 49 feet in length, the narrow Victorian would have been perfect, if only the walls could talk.

"Where do I sign?" I asked the real estate agent that very day. We agreed on a purchase offer. It was meant to be my house, or perhaps I should say, that I was meant to be its temporary custodian. That's how it is with old houses. For all the money and time that you pour into restoring and maintaining the property, the home is never truly your possession. It has its own character. You can only live in it and love it. Then, you must pass it on to new generations.

Two days later, I knew that the only thing separating me from the Victorian was a building inspection. The owner had accepted my bid and agreed to pick up some of the closing costs. I went to my bank, completed the loan application and started packing my belongings in boxes.

Unfortunately, my financial institution turned me down. I couldn't believe it. I had been a member there since I was 16 years old. The large looped handwriting on the bank's registration card proved it. I had the down payment for the house. My salary was modest but I had the monthly housing allowance and my employment was secure. According to my calculation of monthly payments with taxes and insurance premiums, my housing expenses would be roughly the same as the rent I had been paying for the past six years. I had a couple of small credit cards with balances, but I had already paid off two car loans through the bank.

"You've got to be kidding," I said to the manager. "There must be some mistake."

After their rejection, I submitted an application to another bank, which also turned me down. So did the third and fourth financial institutions. Actually, the fourth banker told me that their branch could provide the loan if my parents would co-sign. "What?" I exclaimed. "I'm 40 years old. I have money in the bank, a full-time job, a decent credit history. I am not going to ask my parents to co-sign a loan. Are you out of your ever-loving mind?"

Finally, my real estate friend told me to try Shore Bank. Based in Chicago and African-American owned, the bank gave me a mortgage based on the same information I had provided each of the other financial institutions. No need for a co-signer. No promise of my first-born son. No. They had me sign 50 or 60 forms at closing and gave me a set of keys. If everything goes according to schedule, the charming, $74,000 historic house should be mine to pass on in 30 years.

A House Is Not a Home

Calvin was a pencil-thin, 17-year-old high school dropout. Still, his wardrobe made him look like a grown up. The word 'impeccable' comes to mind to describe his colorful clothing style. Calvin lived in crisp slacks, pressed shirts with coordinated ties, polished dress shoes and, occasionally, donned a wool cap. Calvin never wore blue jeans or sneakers. He didn't own a baseball hat or any of the t-shirts so popular with every other teenager in the continental United States. He was an old soul, and it took me a while to figure out why.

The first Sunday that Calvin attended worship at Cass Church, his eyes kept darting around, as if some gang was chasing him. He sat in the back of the sanctuary, not very far from the door. On Tuesday of the following week, Calvin told our associate pastor, Lamarr Gibson, that he had ended up at Cass by mistake. Evidently a man at the corner store had invited Calvin to his church the week before. Calvin, lousy with directions, ended up off by a block when he wandered into Cass. Hence, Calvin wasn't petrified about becoming a victim of gang violence. He had been looking for the person who invited him to church.

Calvin and Rev. Gibson bonded almost immediately. Rev. Gibson would stop by Calvin's house to offer advice and encouragement to the teen. He brought food, too, once he discovered that Calvin's mother was sick much of the time. When Rev. Gibson was appointed to a new church in Lansing, Calvin was torn about remaining at Cass. Fortunately for the church, he decided to stay. It wasn't long before he began serving as an usher with Ray Travis. Again, he established a close relationship with a man old enough to be his father.

In time, I learned that Calvin had dropped out of school only because his mother's live-in boyfriend forced him to quit. He demanded that Calvin get a full-time job to support the family. Calvin began working at a uniform company about two miles from their house. It was scorching hot, dirty work—dry cleaning and ironing the work outfits. What made it worse was that his mother's boyfriend didn't let Calvin keep any of his earnings. Every other Friday, on payday, the man of the house confiscated Calvin's check after it was signed. He didn't even leave Calvin with money for bus fare. "You're young. You can walk or ride your bike to work," he said sarcastically.

One Friday, after Rev. Gibson was gone, Calvin had had enough. When his mother's boyfriend asked for his wages, Calvin refused to surrender the check. He was as defiant and brave as the college student who willed himself to stand in front of the advancing tanks in Tiananmen Square. His mother's boyfriend didn't utter a word. He retreated into his bedroom, returned with a handgun and held it five inches from Calvin's head. "If you don't give me that GD check," he said, "I'm going to blow your brains all over the wall."

Calvin called me after the incident. He was inconsolable. "OK, here's what we're going to do," I said. "When you are sure that they are both asleep, call me. Let the telephone ring once and then hang up. That will be my signal to come over. I'll pull up in front of the house and wait for you. Pack up just what you need and no more. We can get you new things once you are out of there, but I don't want either of them catching you preparing to leave." All of a sudden, *I* felt as if I was the one who belonged to a gang.

The phone rang just once, shortly after 2 a.m. As I turned the corner onto Temple, I switched off the headlights and silently coasted past the liquor store before stopping in front of Calvin's house. This was well before cell phones, so there was no ability to text. Only doctors had cell phones at that time. I sat in the dark, waiting and wondering if Calvin's mother's boyfriend would blow my brains against the windshield if he found out that I was there to take his paycheck away. Finally, Calvin emerged from the side door with a small duffel bag in tow. He climbed into the car and delicately closed the passenger door. We drove for two blocks before I turned the headlights back on.

At my house, we sat at the dining room table I had inherited from my grandmother, eating Oreos and drinking hot chocolate. (My cure for life's problems is always to break out a healthy snack.) Calvin's rage was palpable. He railed about the boyfriend's addiction. He confessed that he had thought about killing him more than once. Then Calvin said that what made him the angriest about the check episode was his mother. He resented her for not taking his side. "She watched everything and never said a word."

"Maybe she was afraid that if she spoke up, he would take it out on you," I said, knowing by that point that Calvin had a love-hate relationship with his invalid mother.

"No," he burst into tears and buried his head in his shirt sleeve. "She was nodding. She was high."

I pulled out some clean sheets, a blanket and pillow and converted the living room couch into a bed. Calvin slept there for close to three months. The stay gave him the time he needed to sock away enough money to rent a small apartment a stone's throw from the church. He never went home to live again, but he never stopped talking to his mother. She died before Calvin turned 25.

Taking Calvin on trips with the youth, and later the young adults, helped him heal. He was part of the group that traveled to New York. We went to the Apollo Theater one night, and he came undone, laughing uncontrollably, sometimes at inappropriate times, covering his mouth, slapping his leg and waving his arms in the air.

Calvin flew with us to visit Glide Church in San Francisco. We did all the touristy things, like riding the cable cars, shopping at Fisherman's Wharf, touring Alcatraz, eating in Chinatown and taking pictures on Lombard Street. The group even rented bikes and tooled across the Golden Gate Bridge. Calvin liked biking so much that he talked a friend into cycling a second day so they could ride down the crooked street to see if our insurance policy was any good. Another adult had to go with the pair to the rental shop because neither of the adventurers had a credit card to secure the bikes.

In 2003, four of us drove to Washington for a conference on preservation. It was during the hunt for the "D.C. sniper." We were driving an agency van. All of the Cass vehicles are white, just the color the police thought the shooters were driving, and so we joked about being pulled over. In fact, we arrived early, went out for a pancake breakfast, and then met the custodian as he arrived at the National Cathedral. He let us in. Amid the huge liturgical banners and intricate carved figures, Calvin and one of the other team members lay down and fell asleep. After our trip, every time the Cathedral held a televised service—the memorial for the victims of 9/11, the funeral for Dorothy Height, the memorial for Neil Armstrong—Calvin would call me up and ask if I remembered being there.

Now 30-something, Calvin still dresses immaculately. He has shaved his head bald and wears a slight mustache and a few chin hairs, like Will Smith in the movie *Hitch*. Calvin is a movie buff. About the only things he loves more than movies are music and dancing. At Cass, we encourage people to dance during worship service while we sing the birthday song. Calvin struts and sways and claps his hands all the way down the center aisle on his birthday. He is kind. He likes "big women"— his phrase, not mine. And he still misses his mother.

Send in Suze Orman

Early on, the Cass Finance Office looked more like a room than a department. Just two people handled everything to do with money—deposits, bank reconciliations, 13 checkbooks, accounts receivable, accounts payable and audits. This was well before QuickBooks or Sarbanes-Oxley. Generally, with just two people, we were a day late and a dollar short. Beyond that, there was a constant flow of staff visitors who wanted help with financial matters related to their programs.

Rick Murry headed up the department. Rick was a retired executive from the train industry. He tended to be low-key and understated with an extremely dry sense of humor. One day his staff member made a crack about a certain bill collector having PMS and all the women waiting in the office howled with laughter. It was a way of letting off steam, but the minute they remembered that Rick was present and that he might not think the joke was funny, the laughing stopped abruptly.

"It's not a problem," he assured them. "I get PMS." The hilarity resumed louder than before. A couple of the women doubled over. One giggled and another openly snorted.

"Rick," I said, thinking that maybe he didn't know what the acronym meant, "you can't get PMS."

"Sure, I get it," he responded without missing a beat. "It's like second hand smoke."

Then the women in the room became hysterical. Rick never cracked a smile, but if you looked down at the stomach section of his dress shirt, you could see his belly thumping up and down with amusement.

This brings up two things: nonprofits generally have more women employees than men. There are a number of theories as to why this is so but whatever the reason, the result is a different work culture. Also, Cass has been extremely fortunate over the years to attract and employ retirees who were conscientious workers like Rick and who brought a wealth of experience from former jobs.

God knows we needed it. We were receiving daily threats—to turn off our utilities, to repossess our vehicles, to start litigation, to contact the bishop or the media or both. There were stacks of intimidating letters. Cass was on autodial with a fair number of collection agencies. Shut-off notices were regularly posted on the church doors, like Luther's 95 Theses in Wittenberg. The finance staff struggled just to keep enough money in the accounts to meet payroll every other week. Once wages and the payroll taxes were satisfied, Rick moved on to cover utilities and then insurance. Anything after that was a bonus.

For the first five months, payroll didn't include me. It was OK. I tend to be frugal, conservative with money, and had socked away enough to live on temporarily. Eventually the agency caught up with the back wages, but it would be years before they started paying on my pension. So I began thinking about how I could create a retirement nest egg, in case Cass was never able to contribute to the pension program. When the duplex next door to my house went up for sale, I decided that it would suffice as a retirement asset. I purchased the 1920-something brick building, with its in-ground swimming pool and the adjacent lot that would provide off-street parking for the duplex tenants. On the back of the same lot, there was also a turn-of-the-century carriage house that had undoubtedly belonged to my house originally. Its function would have been to accommodate the Esterling family's carriages, horses, tack and hay. At some point before I purchased the carriage house, there had been a fire in the two-story brick structure. Still, it had plenty of character, and I had hopes of renovating it into a guesthouse for small volunteer teams.

I tried using the carriage house as a garage for the two properties. I locked lawn tools and lawn mowers inside. Unfortunately, six lawn mowers were stolen in three years. Crooks came right over the eight-foot tall, stockade-style fence, cut off the locks with bolt cutters and hoisted the machines up and over. They even stole used mowers. The two properties were simply too large to cut with a push mower, therefore I eventually moved the lawn mower inside my house. Specifically, it was relocated to my kitchen. Given how infrequently I use the kitchen, it wasn't a huge problem. Friends often commented about the mower, but I really didn't pay them much attention. During the winter months, I simply moved the machine to the basement. I needed the space for the snow blower. It fit nicely in front of the dishwasher.

The biggest immediate benefit of owning the duplex next door was that it provided a community swimming pool. A large number of city kids don't know how to swim, a lesson I learned after taking a group to an area wave pool and watching one of our frantic junior high students fished up out of the water by a lifeguard. Ever since I purchased the duplex, we have been able to take a busload of Cass children swimming on Friday afternoons throughout the summer. The first Friday is always memorable.

"OK. Hang up your towels and put on a life jacket," the drill starts. "Wear your shoes any time you are outside of the pool gate, because the yard has random dog poop and pieces of glass. No running. No diving face first. No pushing. The pool is only four and a half feet deep. The teenagers from whatever place is volunteering this week will be in the water with you if you need help. Have fun and stay safe."

Two or three will actually jump into the cold water at that point. Eight or 10 will sit on the cement lip that goes around the pool, swinging their naked legs and feet in the water. The last bunch will plant themselves on the steps that descend into the pool. Members of the visiting youth group will try to coax the stair crew in. "Jump, I'll catch you." "Here's a kick board." "What's your name again? I have a cousin with that name, too." Someone will offer to provide a piggyback ride, and eventually one of the smaller children will climb on. Most end up leaving the steps by taking the rider route. The human horse teams will race before long. One or two hesitant swimmers will opt to be circlers—hanging on to the rim of the pool and moving along the wall hand over hand. When one runs into another circler coming from the opposite direction, the two will go one way so that neither will have to let go of the edge.

As the afternoon pool party goes on, balls begin to fly through the air. Kids and teens play catch and keep-away, until someone decides to throw a ball up for a second person to catch in midair while jumping into the water. Goggles are applied to those daring to swim underwater. A teenager will do the dead man's float and another child unfamiliar with water activities starts to yell, "HE'S DROWNING!" The head of every adult spins around to visually check for trouble.

No one drowns. The group slows down the first day. Shelter kids rarely get as much play and exercise time as they deserve. They emerge from the now-milky waters smiling and happy, except for the fact that they have to stop. We bribe them with popsicles or juice boxes after hanging up their red life jackets and drying off. Almost every Friday someone loses a shirt or sock. The lost-and-found grows to be the size of a small department store. "Can we come back next week, Rev. Fowler?"

"As long as the weather is good," I respond. They repeat the question every Friday. The last swim opportunity of the summer will be an all-day affair. It takes us forever to get them out of the water. Once they emerge, they look like raisins for the next half hour.

The group returns to Cass on the bus. The visiting youth depart, too. I let my dog outside after being cooped inside with the lawnmower all day. Then, I add enough chlorine to the pool to kill a horse as I thank God for an investment property that seems like a piece of paradise.

And the Walls Came Tumbling Down

It was 15 minutes before I was scheduled to speak to 2,500 teenagers in Springfield, Missouri, when a message arrived from one of my duplex tenants. The text was primarily a photo. It appeared foggy because the picture had been taken through a misty storm door window. Still, there was no problem distinguishing the bulldozer, smashing through the exterior wall of my carriage house with its powerful metal blade. Underneath the shot was one sentence: "Did you know about this?" I did not.

I called the sender straight away. "What is happening?" I demanded to know. The college-aged resident explained that a massive bulldozer had arrived about 20 minutes prior and that it was demolishing the 100-year-old structure. The second story of the red brick carriage house was already heaped on the ground. The contents of the historic structure had been instantly rendered useless.

Two weeks before the out-of-state youth conference gig, I discovered a business card tucked between my front doors at home. The beige card contained the name, title, address and telephone number of a representative from the city. In blue ink, someone had crossed out the printed telephone number and wrote a new number with the words, "Call between eight and 10 a.m." That was it. I telephoned on five different weekday mornings. No one ever answered and, although there was a message after the initial ringing, the recording indicated that the voicemail wasn't set up and that it was not possible to leave a message. Were the two things connected? I was unsure.

I walked out through a massive curtain into the arena-like room. The podium was positioned in front of a drum set and a number of guitars, arranged for the bands that would perform later. I had trouble seeing the audience due to the intense flood lights bathing the stage. My message explained why works are important for people of faith and why youth groups should consider volunteering in Detroit. The T-shirt clad crowd was warm and receptive. Still, I had trouble concentrating. Fortunately, Gladys and the Ambassadors choir were next. They brought high energy. The youth were on their feet.

Then, the men and I led separate workshops for the Missouri teenagers before we piled into our minibus. I was relieved to be back in the driver's seat, with the group but artificially isolated, alone to deal with my rage. My house and duplex were surrounded by vacant, scrapper-trashed structures. The city itself owned countless dangerous, abandoned buildings that stood open to both the elements and the public—schools, police precincts, fire stations. Why did they level the carriage house? Detroit notoriously had thousands of homes and businesses that were delinquent on their taxes. Why did they pick a parcel that was current with property taxes? The carriage house needed renovations but it was secured. The grass was cut. I shoveled the snow all winter. It just didn't make sense. The bulldozer came right through the wall, as unwelcome as the crooks who had entered the church using a pickup truck to steal our meat years before. The city had contracted with a company to come onto my property and smash something that I owned without notice, without a hearing, without a posting, without caring, I was absolutely livid behind the wheel. It felt as if gravity was gone. Predictability itself had been destroyed for me.

Friends and neighbors got word of the destruction and they called to urge me to alert the media. A few advised me to lawyer-up and sue the city. Like Job's friends, their intentions were good and they began by trying to console me. It only made me conclude that they didn't understand my relationship with the city. I loved it and hated it simultaneously. Moreover, Cass was a recipient of city funding and that complicated everything. We drove from Springfield, Missouri to performances in Kansas City, then to a small church pastored by a seminary friend in Iowa and, finally, north to Wisconsin and Illinois. I gradually began to sort the incident out in my mind.

As the Cass vehicle crawled along the highway, I remembered others who probably experienced similar emotions as their houses and businesses were seized for expressways. Chinatown was razed for the Lodge freeway. Interstate 75 severed Mexican town by bisecting Bagley Street. I-96 cut right through the middle of African American homes congregated along Grand River on the west side and I-94 took a swath of the northern section of Paradise Valley.

Eminent domain had been used too, to confiscate 1,200 homes, 140 businesses and several churches in order to build the General Motors Poletown assembly plant. Even Mayor Coleman Young supported the action. An old union man, Young sided with the company because he was desperate for city jobs. In fact, the facility that straddles the Detroit-Hamtramck border has employed large numbers of people since it opened in 1985. How do you decide what is and what isn't the common good? Three hundred homes in the Delray area were slated to be taken and razed by the state in order to build a second bridge to Canada.

I hadn't lost my house, even if I hadn't been properly notified. I was angry that the world had become arbitrary. For the first time, my rights had been trampled and my innocence died. Slowly, I understood that this was the world poor people occupy and that I am only there voluntarily.

I could have used our media connections to broadcast the story, Al Sharpton style. Half of my friends were lawyers who would have taken the case pro-bono. I had the money and people to install a temporary fence and the credit to erect an eight-foot wooden one to permanently bridge the new alley gap. This was not the end of the world. I was not powerless. I was not poor. Unlike others, I could walk away any time I wanted. Perhaps for the first time, I thought I should.

Then, a few minutes prior to the last tour concert, late morning in Evanston, Illinois, my nephew called to tell me that my mother had died. Again, I was a wreck as our function began. Gladys and the men, exhausted by the endless travel, performed exceptionally well. Sue Pethoud, our Church and Community staff member, engaged the crowd with the skill of Dale Carnegie.

Once we were back in Detroit, I started sifting through the rubble. The clean-up would require a year and a half, even with the substantial help from volunteer teams, who worked like human mules. Using two wheelbarrows and an endless supply of shovels, masks and gloves, we moved at least 20,000 bricks and filled 12 huge construction dumpsters with debris before it was done. The process gave me a new appreciation for the Israelites, who were forced to make bricks with no straw, and an opportunity to grieve.

Ultimately, I learned from someone high in the Bing administration that the city had mailed me two notices, but that they were both returned as "undeliverable." Another duplex neighbor indicated that an inspector had knocked on her door the Friday night before the Saturday demolition. He indicated that they couldn't contact me. He told her that the carriage house had to be demolished because the city had a grant that it needed to spend down to satisfy a deadline. She responded that I had plans to renovate the building, but then she forgot to relay the conversation to me. Some things defy logic.

Obviously, I stayed.

On the Road Again

"Vacationary" is the term coined by people who are critical of church mission trips. Their primary argument against short-term mission excursions is based on money. The detractors point out that the funds raised and spent on travel and food for the team could be better used to hire local laborers or to buy needed materials. They make a legitimate point. If a youth group spends $3,000 or $4,000 to journey somewhere else to paint a room or two, it doesn't make economic sense. If the group sent the same amount to hire local painters to do the job, unemployed or underemployed people would have work and they would probably spend their earnings in the neighborhood helping to support local commerce. There's a high probability that professional painters could accomplish more and would do a better job (and wouldn't waste supplies by having a paint fight).

Still, I am a believer in most short-term mission experiences, whether they involve joining existing agencies or responding to a natural disaster. Traveling together fosters nurturing relationships between the participants and, when the volunteers are youth, between young people and the adults who accompany them. I have had more crucial conversations with kids while I am driving and they are riding shotgun than I have ever had in my office or a Sunday school room.

Road trips invite talk. Someone is having trouble at school. Someone is in love. Someone's parents are getting divorced or remarried. Someone isn't sure she or he believes in God. Someone says for the first time that she or he wants to serve God. These are million dollar conversations. And the kids have them with the other adults, too, and lifelong friendships are forged.

The best mission trips also allow for important dialogue and relationships with the people at the destination. At Cass, this includes the staff, such as Willie and Lynette and Shorty and Nicki and Bobby in the food program. It's hotter than Hades in the kitchen by 10 a.m., but the staff will have the groups singing, dancing, joking and talking all while they crank out thousands of meals. In the warehouse, Ed, Stacy, Karen and Geneal are rock stars. They get the groups to finish so much work as they joke around and openly discuss ultimate things – God, grace, race, sin, sex, college, climate change and a host of other hot potato topics.

Especially in the warehouse, the volunteers get to know people who have been homeless. They work shoulder to shoulder with the formerly homeless men and women who serve as the teachers and experts. In the process, the youth have permission to ask anything, and the Green Industries' employees know that they can choose whether or not to answer. I am always amazed at their candor. By the end of the week, the teenagers have helped with recycling, but beyond that they got to know someone, or several someones, who have been homeless and unemployed. The youth have learned about mental illness and drug abuse firsthand. It's not a cop lecturing them to stay away from narcotics: they know an addict who shared how abusing drugs negatively impacted everything. These are also priceless conversations.

You might be surprised to learn that we do mission trips from Cass. Having taken groups to Appalachia and Mountain T.O.P. in Tennessee and a Native American program in New Mexico in the past, I knew the value of trips. Plus, since Cass receives so many visiting mission teams in a year, I want us always to be mindful of what groups have had to do to travel to Detroit and what good hospitality looks like, and feels like. We rotate our mission trips. One year, we take an adult team and the next year belongs to the youth. Cass groups have gone to Ohio, Florida, New York, Texas, and Massachusetts. One adult team went to Puerto Rico and another flew to Zimbabwe to volunteer at the Old Mutarre Mission.

The Africa trip was so important for me personally because it helped me frame so many of my ideas about poverty. Poor people in Detroit don't have the basic necessities, even if they have a job. They tend to lack adequate food, reliable transportation, needed medication and decent housing. They routinely have their lights, gas and water turned off. Safety is an issue. Education is deficient. Poverty in Zimbabwe meant many of the same problems, and yet poor people there had additional obstacles.

The Cass team worked at the orphanage and the hospital because we had a nurse practitioner in our group. One day, a new patient arrived, folded up in a shopping cart. His relative had pushed him in the plastic cart for five miles over dirt paths. Once the pair arrived, they waited for the part-time doctor to turn up. Then, the healthy man walked the same distance back to town to get the prescription filled because the hospital didn't have a pharmacy. No roads. No ambulance. One part-time physician. Poverty isn't good in either place, but first world and third world poverty aren't identical.

Another reason the trips are critical for us is that so many members of our community don't travel. The kids who went to Boston ate lobster for the very first time, and they were astonished to discover that the ocean "smelled." If you have only seen pictures of the Atlantic, how would you know about the scent? When we stopped at a gorge during the New England tour, one of the men refused to get off the bus because he was afraid we would be attacked by bears. He had never been to a national park. In Puerto Rico, the team visited the rainforest and brought back a picture to hang in the warehouse for the Green Industries employees to appreciate. In the middle of Iowa farmland, we stopped at a gas station with a Subway sandwich shop and, after inquiring where we were from, the matronly woman behind the counter asked the group if they would sing something for her. It turned into an impromptu performance, and the other patrons, all of them rural white people, sang along to music of the Temptations and Stevie Wonder.

Six months after Hurricane Katrina, Cass Church organized a team to work in Biloxi, MS, through the United Methodist Committee on Relief (UMCOR). Eight of us drove south. Half of the group assisted a family living in a FEMA trailer, and my group worked with a family still residing in their storm-damaged home. Gloria, Esther, Keith and I spent the week removing black mold. We were prepared for the grimy task with work gloves, masks, safety glasses and scrapers. Once the walls were clean, we applied 15 gallons of Kilz. It was nasty work interrupted only by conversations with the family members.

After a week of physical labor, our team drove to New Orleans for a barbeque dinner with a member of Cass who was stationed there as a FEMA consultant, before heading back to Michigan. On the way home, we stopped in Tennessee. A couple of the adults wanted to see Graceland. Elvis' home was lit up, but it was closed to the public, we were told, because Priscilla was hosting a private event. So, instead we drove to a cheesy souvenir shop to check out the velvet pictures, t-shirts, mugs and key chains of the king of rock-n-roll.

Most of the group went inside while I stayed with the packed van. When two of the team members returned, I headed into the shop to use the restroom. There was Gloria standing directly in front of the counter clerk. Her arms were crossed, elbows pointing up toward the ceiling, hands clinching her shirt, which was hoisted up to her neck. Her torso was naked and her entire bra was exposed. "What is going on?" I demanded.

"He said I stole a book," she stated, obviously shaken and embarrassed. Gloria had raised her top to convince his accuser that she hadn't taken anything. "I picked up a couple of things to look at them but I didn't steal anything."

"Hell, no. Pull your top down," I snapped. I was appalled. "She didn't steal any book. We're on the way home from a mission trip. This woman spent the better part of last week removing mold from a stranger's home that had been hammered by Katrina's winds and waves. Come on, let's go, Gloria."

I yanked her by the wrist as soon as her blouse was back in place.

The employee didn't issue an apology, nor did he call the police. As we made a beeline back to the van, Gloria grabbed my arm and said, "You know I didn't take anything that didn't belong to me, Rev. Fowler, especially not that Elvis Presley stuff."

It would have been funny if I hadn't been infuriated.

Although I go on regular vacations, Cass trips offer me a change of perspective. It really doesn't matter whether we have been headed south or north, east or west. When the Cass youth went to Massachusetts, the group was re-directed to a hotel that accommodated only people of color. In upstate New York, a gas station clerk threatened to call the police on us for using what he claimed to be a counterfeit bill when the Ambassadors came in to buy pop and cigarettes.

Driving with black people is not the same thing as driving while black, but it certainly is not the same as traveling with an all-white group. Each episode of harassment has been eye-opening for me. I have been reminded that people of other races and religions still receive very different, discriminating treatment when they leave home and that everyone deserves to know that the ocean smells and that you can see the stars best in a rural black sky. These glimpses of bigotry

are one of the reasons I am a huge supporter of trips, mission
and otherwise.

That Still, Small Voice

One of the perks of my job is driving our newest vehicles before they rack up too many miles. In 2008, that meant taking the agency's Ford Escape hybrid to Arlington, Virginia, for a conference. Although I generally fly to accumulate frequent-flier miles, our board chair had agreed to accompany me to the session, thus driving was a better use of our funds. What's more, driving would allow us, both history buffs, to visit Abraham Lincoln's summer cottage at the Soldiers' Home while we were in the area.

It was late in the afternoon when we left Detroit. The SUV still had that new car smell. Sue explored the gadgets while I navigated the rush hour traffic. The vehicle was loaded with power windows and locks, heated seats, a moon roof, an over-the-top sound system and even plug-in options for your laptop. I suggested to my travel companion that we engage the Garmin navigation system to have a general idea of how many miles and hours we needed to travel.

As we drove south on I-75, Garmin Girl's voice began issuing instructions, but the volume was faint, almost a whisper. "What is she saying?" I asked Sue. "Can you turn it up slightly?"

Sue punched several combinations of buttons, but the GPS voice remained at an annoyingly low level. My partner in crime twisted knobs, blasted the music on the radio and then silenced it. It was a futile attempt. Finally Sue lowered her head next to the dashboard speaker, perching it in place and tilting until she resembled the dog listening to the phonograph cylinder on the RCA record label. Still no luck.

"Maybe it's a defect," Sue concluded.

"Why don't you grab the owner's manual and see if that will help," I suggested, frustrated that we might need to know what she was telling us.

"I can't read while I'm riding," she answered. "It makes me puke."

"Never mind," I responded quickly, gagging a little just thinking about her vomiting next to me. Did we pay for Scotchgard? I wondered, but I said, "That's OK, we can read it when we stop for gas."

I took my eyes off the road momentarily to pick up my cold drink when I noticed that the magenta line on the small display map was lit up with bright white flashing arrows. "I think it's trying to tell us to get off. It looks like Garmin Girl wants us to take I-94 to 23 south. That doesn't make any sense," I said. In fact, using that route would have added at least another hour to the trip and we were under the gun as it was. We needed to shave off time, not pick up another 60 minutes.

"Don't look at the screen," Sue advised and all I could think of was, "Pay no attention to the man behind the curtain." Those arrows prompted us for hours.

We were oblivious to the screen in short order. The two of us were busy catching up with one another. We had junk food to consume and songs to sing. Occasionally we joked about the woman's muffled voice, but that was it.

Did I mention that the Escape was a hybrid? We didn't pull off for gas until we reached Langley, Virginia. Sue went into the service station and I grabbed the manual out of the glove compartment. It was still wrapped in cellophane. After reading the instructions, I manipulated the proper knob and heard the woman scream, "GET OFF! GET OFF! GET OFF! Recalculating. GET OFF! GET OFF!" I was surprised that she didn't have laryngitis after 500 miles. Using the manual, I ascertained that someone somewhere had programmed the GPS preferences to avoid highways. Garmin Girl had tried her best.

When I explained what had happened to Sue, she burst out laughing and sprayed her mouthful of food everywhere. I could barely see to drive for the tears streaming down my face.

In retrospect, there were plenty of lessons learned before we set foot in the seminar—read the instructions before you start the engine, stop and turn up the volume of muted voices, expect every trip to include some trouble, be sure to take a friend, and drive a hybrid because it provides unbelievable fuel efficiency.

Having solved the GPS puzzle on the way to Arlington, Sue and I stopped at Lincoln's Cottage before heading back to Detroit. The landmark occupies a hill overlooking downtown Washington. The president and Mary Lincoln sought sanctuary there after the death of their son, Willie. I'm told that Lincoln spent summer nights there as well to escape the heat and humidity of Washington, D.C. It offered no retreat from the war, however. Just four months after the start of the Civil War, a national cemetery was established next to the residence. The Commander-in-Chief witnessed the sounds and sight of the daily Union soldier burials. It was with that backdrop that Lincoln penned the preliminary draft of the Emancipation Proclamation. He must have taught himself how to block out the constant distractions so he could hear that still, small voice that we so often ignore.

Pancreatic Cancer

It was the end of a long day and I was still in a skirt and heels finishing a "What's new at Cass?" spiel at Birmingham First United Methodist Church. Birmingham is everything that Cass is not. The suburb is affluent and vibrant. The houses are huge with attractive landscaping. The Birmingham Church building is hospital-clean. The congregation is large, composed primarily of professionals and corporate executives, who run businesses in the tri-county area and take jets to India and China and Chile like the rest of us might jump in the car or on the bus to go to the grocery store. And still, this group of global deciders is committed to a partnership with Cass and a gaggle of other nonprofit groups. If CEO is their title, mission is their middle name.

As with almost every engagement I have ever done, after speaking, I invited questions from the listeners. Audience queries tend to be predictable. What do you think about corruption in the city government? Should I give money to panhandlers? Isn't poverty worse in other countries? Have you ever considered selling the Cass Tiffany windows to minister to the poor? Is your dog's middle name really Lucifer? Does Cass have a wish list of needed items? But on this particular night in Birmingham, an elderly woman caught me off guard with a new one.

She looked rather innocent. Certainly she was someone's grandmother and probably a long-time member of the suburban congregation. She was petite and polite. Her question was as masterfully framed as a painting in the Louvre.

"Rev. Fowler, I went to hear the orchestra a short time ago. After the concert, I was returning to my car and I saw a small group of prostitutes standing on the corner near your church. What have you done about the prostitutes?" she asked.

Having graduated at the top of my class from the seminary of sarcasm, I wasted no time in responding. "Well ma'am," I said, "I've taught them to tithe."

That's not what I wanted to say, of course. I wanted to answer in rapid succession:

Right after I secured peace in the Middle East, discovered a cure for pancreatic cancer, reversed global warming, eliminated hunger and obesity, abolished unemployment, eradicated homelessness and purged the country of racism and sexism and the obscene income disparity, then I eliminated the oldest profession on the planet.

I was stunned by her question.

Are you kidding me? What have I done about the prostitutes? She had no idea what she was asking or how long I had struggled with the do-everything litmus test. As a perfectionist, a pastor and a woman, I am wired to make everything right and to care for everyone else. And being a Christian doesn't help. Jesus is always challenging us to leave everyone (even your dead father) and love everyone (even those who persecute you) and give everything (like the widow with her mite) and leave everything (take no staff, no bag, nor bread, nor money, not even two tunics—I'm sure he'd approve of a pair of Detroit Treads though).

At the conclusion of so many days, you feel like Oskar Schindler at the end of WWII. An unlikely hero initially, he had spent an inordinate amount of time and money bribing SS guards and Nazi officers, including the commandant of Auschwitz, in an effort to save his Jewish workers. When the end was certain, Schindler had to escape the advancing Red Army because he was both a member of the Nazi Party and a war profiteer. Before he departed, his workers made a ring for him, using the gold from a man's bridgework. They engraved a verse in Hebrew from the Talmud which can be paraphrased: "Whoever saves one life saves the entire world." Schindler was moved by this sacrificial gesture, yet it caused him to be unsettled and ashamed that he hadn't done more.

What have I done about the prostitutes? I said to myself as the others were enjoying refreshments. While I haven't done anything about prostitutes in the abstract, Cass has helped plenty of women, many who have sold themselves at one time or another. The truth is that I can't do everything.

She Works Hard
For Her Money

"Tippy Toes" was a prolific prostitute in the Cass Corridor. There are two versions of how Betty Jean got her nickname. The first was related to the high-heeled cowboy boots that she always wore. They fit Tippy Toes' scrawny legs loosely the way those yellow rain boots did back in the 1960s—first hitting the front of your legs before smacking the backs of them as you walked. It was the height of the boot heels, though, that made it necessary for her to walk on her tiptoes.

The second story was that Tippy Toes was a heroin addict who shot up using the soles of her feet, consequently she couldn't walk flat on the ground.

Tippy Toes considered herself a functioning addict. She would show up at Cass for worship some Sundays and religiously announce during the Joys and Concerns time that she had quit using drugs a few days prior. The congregation always broke into spontaneous, encouraging applause.

One morning, most of my extended family had joined us for a baptism. Following her sobriety proclamation, I watched her scurry straightaway over to their pews where she tried to hustle them for cash. None of my relatives responded with money, so she moved on to others to support her habit. I lost track of her visually for a period as the service continued, but then I spied Tippy Toes as she darted into the closest bathroom. At 45, she relapsed once again.

Shortly after that Sunday, her disappearance was more permanent. Rumors circulated that she had passed away. That often happened. Most of the time there was no way of knowing. Many prostitutes and homeless people change their "addresses" as frequently as most people launder their bed sheets. Until recently, they didn't carry cell phones. What's more, often they don't want you to have their contact information because their relationships with their families have disintegrated. All of this is to say that there is no way to know and no one to ask. Even when you are sure that someone has died, frequently there is no way to notify the family. Like undeliverable mail, hundreds of bodies lie unclaimed in the county morgue.

I checked with the hospitals first. Then, I moved on to DPD's Homicide Division and finally the Wayne County Medical Examiner's Office. No Betty Jean. No Tippy Toes. It was a couple of years later that I ran into her at the 36th District Court. She looked so much better. Her ruddy complexion glowed. Her clean hair was professionally dyed and styled. She had gained some healthy weight. She was obviously no longer under the grip of drugs.

Betty explained that she had blown through an inheritance from her mother's estate and that the experience had practically killed her. Using an economy of words, she continued, "My friends who aren't in prison are dead. I would be too if I hadn't gone into rehab in Macomb County."

She told me that she was just in court to take care of some outstanding accosting & soliciting (prostitution) warrants. She didn't recognize me. I said I was from Cass Church and I invited her to come back. "Everyone would love to see you," I said.

Betty replied that she couldn't return to the Corridor. "The neighborhood has too many triggers for me. I don't think I can dodge the addiction bullet again."

Carla was another story altogether. I was sitting in my office at the church that very first year. It was almost Christmas and I was ready to quit. The debt. The grants. The audits. The staff. The poor. The donors. I was a mess, ready to call the bishop to request a circuit—four or five congregations—in the Upper Peninsula, when a knock came at the door. Actually, the person beat on the door as if it were a bass drum.

Because I had gone to the finest seminary in the country, where they taught us about empathy and sympathy, compassion and counseling, "seeing Jesus" in the poor and "entertaining angels unaware," I yelled just before the birth of Jesus, "Go away, I'm busy." In fact, I was agitated by the interruption. A Mt. Kilimanjaro-pile of paperwork awaited my attention or signature.

The intruder was not fazed. The banging began to sound like a battering ram. Every pound caused the door to shake in its frame, as if the person behind it was saying, *I don't care how ugly you are, I'm going to stand here and pelt this door until you let me in.* Then, because Boston University equipped its grads with emotional intelligence and an "as you did it unto the least of these" theology, I screamed, "All right then, come in!" It was a good thing it wasn't the district superintendent.

The door swung open ever so slowly and there on the other side was Carla. Like Tippy Toes, even if I hadn't recognized her, I would have quickly guessed her occupation immediately. She was every bit the television stereotype. Dressed in spandex tight pants with a loud, low-cut top, a leather coat and thick make-up, Carla was drenched in perfume. It really didn't matter what she was wearing, though; customers were eager and willing to pay just about any street prostitute $10 a half hour in the alley behind my church.

Without entering the office, Carla pointed her index finger at my face. "Rev. Fowler, you've … got … to … get … her … off … my … corner!" she demanded, pausing after every word.

Wow, I thought to myself, *I knew the bishop had given me authority, I just never realized how far it extended.*

I looked up. Like one of the emaciated children cowering by the Ghost of Christmas Present, a girl, just 12 years old, was in Carla's clutch. At that moment, despite all the excellent education that I have been privileged to receive, I couldn't think of a thing to say. I summoned one of our caseworkers to call her parents and notify the authorities. My eyes followed them as the pre-teen was escorted out of the office. Then, Carla and I sat there alone on opposite sides of my desk. She spoke quietly and I will never forget what she said. "You know, Rev. Fowler, I wasn't so much worried about losing business, but when I looked at that little girl, I saw myself and I knew that the church could save her."

The image of the child standing by my door and Carla's words spoken at my desk have been etched into my soul. On days that I think I'm too busy to be bothered, they shame me.

Epilogue

"Are things getting better in the city?" or "What's next?" are the two things others ask routinely. The first question is the result of people being curious about Detroit after a mayoral transition or since Emergency Financial Manager Kevyn Orr filed for bankruptcy. The later query comes because people recognize that Cass is always on the lookout for new and better ways to solve problems. I want to finish by talking about some of the under-reported developments in Detroit and one of the next programs at Cass.

Detroit is changing in some exciting ways. It is reinventing itself even as others are stuck in reciting the litany of negative changes that began in the 1950s. Take development for example. In the last 20 years, Hudson's Department Store was imploded and Tiger Stadium was razed, but during the same period, the Gem Theater was moved a few blocks rather than demolished. Comerica Park was built. Ford Field developed and the Lions came back to the city. Plans for a new $650 million arena complex are underway for the Red Wings, too.

Campus Martius was re-developed into an urban oasis complete with a fountain, sculptures and the "point of origin" plaque. Visit during the winter and the 1.2-acre park will remind you of Rockefeller Center with a crowded ice rink. Thousands of people enjoy the Motown Winter Blast there. Come in the summer and you will hear jazz bands or watch movies at night projected on a giant screen. Have dinner at the

Hard Rock Café. It's now tucked into the Compuware Building across the street. Spend the night at what was the Book Cadillac Hotel (now the Westin Book Cadillac hotel). It reopened after a $200-million reconstruction project.

Transportation is changing, as well. Senior citizens still talk about the good old days when they traveled by streetcar and train. As I write, the M-1 Rail is under construction on Woodward Avenue, and hopefully, it will eventually extend to the neighborhoods beyond downtown, Midtown and New Center. People in the neighborhoods need dependable, affordable and safe regional mass transit.

A quiet revolution has occurred in the last decade. A biking culture now permeates Detroit. When the potholes are repaired and the streets are repaved, bike lanes are included for people to pedal to and from work. What's more, a section of the Grand Trunk Western Railroad line has been converted into the Dequindre Cut, a dedicated cycling path that begins at Mack, runs along Eastern Market and ends at the riverfront south of Jefferson Avenue. If you didn't know it, you'd think you were in Amsterdam rather than Detroit. Those without wheels can even rent bikes from stands around the city. On Monday nights, thousands of people participate in long, leisurely group bike rides through the city thanks to Slow Roll co-founders Jason Hall and Mike MacKool. This would have been unthinkable 20 years back.

The composition of residents has changed. Everyone has written about the depopulation of the city, but new people are arriving. The influx of transplants from southern states and European countries has virtually stopped, but Hispanic and Middle Eastern immigrants are choosing southeastern Michigan and Detroit in record numbers. They add to the area's already rich diversity. Michigan's Republican governor has even set a goal of attracting 50,000 immigrants to help repopulate the city in the next five years, given their strong drive, solid work ethic and entrepreneurial skills. This is a radical change.

Young adults are moving into Detroit once again, too. They are educated, energetic and ambitious. Scores of them are artists and business leaders. Quicken Loans' Dan Gilbert deserves a great deal of credit for luring thousands of young professionals to work and live in the D. Occasionally these young adults rub the old-time residents the wrong way by implying that they have come to "save" the city, but no one can argue that there is room enough for everyone in Detroit. Certainly everyone benefits from the income taxes and property taxes paid by the latest arrivals. They also benefit the larger community by shopping, entertaining and frequently providing leadership in the community.

Are there still urgent issues? Absolutely. How many of the young people will stay once they have school-aged children? The Detroit Public School system is in disarray, under its fourth consecutive appointed Emergency Manager. DPS dropout and force-out rates are appalling. The charter schools, which were touted as the answer to the public education system, aren't performing measurably better. Private schools and parochial schools are expensive, and suburban schools require travel time. Change can't come soon enough for education in the city.

The drug trade and its related violence continue to plague Detroit. Every week, citizens are gunned down in drug-related crimes. Store clerks are robbed. Drivers are car-jacked. Children are shot for their shoes. Innocent victims are gunned down on porches. Occasionally, little ones are killed when stray bullets or firebombs penetrate their homes. For years people protested so that folks wouldn't be confined to the back of a bus, but today we remain largely silent as our citizens, many of them children, are put in the back of a hearse.

Sam Cooke's song promises that "a change is gonna come." Let it be so.

The economy itself is changing. The recession taught us all about the volatility of the stock market, the instability of mortgages and foreclosure, banking bailouts and bankruptcy. We have also been properly schooled about the shrinking middle class, CEO compensation and the ever-expanding gap between the rich and the poor. Pundits frequently talk about the "new normal." What they mean is that the American Dream is over.

We are living in a post-industrial time. Automobile plants no longer employ large numbers of people in Detroit or throughout our state. Still, we made products prior to cars, trucks and tanks. At the beginning of the last century, Detroit was distinguished for manufacturing freighters. We made stoves. We were the third largest producer of tobacco products. Some thought the right change was to switch from manufacturing to gambling, but a casino-economy is not the answer to employment or commerce.

Still, there has been a positive change in Detroit. We're hand-making watches and bikes at Shinola. Detroit Denim is producing blue jeans. Tech Town is steadily launching new startups. Area gardens are selling fresh produce at Eastern Market. Stroh's has been replaced by Atwater Brewery. Trendy new restaurants have popped up, like the Green Dot Stables and Slows Bar-B-Q. Some existing large businesses have moved back into the city, too, like Compuware and, more recently, the Lowe Campbell Ewald advertising firm.

Detroit is open for business.

Cass Community has changed dramatically. You have read about new affordable housing and the pedestrian campus, food production and job creation. Naturally, not every idea has worked. Some of our innovations have proved as useless as wet spaghetti on the floor that wouldn't stick to the wall. Still, we believe that adaption and change and risk-taking are synonymous with survival.

The grassroots Cass Community Publishing House (CCPH) is what's next. It is the reason behind this book. We needed to understand all things publishing—copy editing, content editing, choosing titles, fact checking, typesetting, cover design, selection of paper and methods of binding and ISBN registration.

Fortunately, we have incredible teachers with David Crumm and his David Crumm Media staff. They are on top of the substantial changes in the publishing world, like books on demand (so that there is no need to print or store inventory) and the advent of electronic versions of books for people who prefer a paperless volume. They, of course, have a solid handle on marketing and distribution.

The thrilling element for us is the ability to give unique voices and underrepresented perspectives a legitimate outlet. Self-publishing is costly and lacks the rigor of an editing process. Conversely, the top five or six English-language publishers rarely invest in new authors. I tell folks that CCPH wants to be "the" publishing house that puts out quality work that will expose readers to another view of the world like *The Red Tent*, *The Kite Runner*, *The Help* or *The Butler*. Some of the books will be religious; others will not. We expect to solicit authors to write history, biography, poetry and fiction. I doubt that we'll do science fiction, but you never know.

There is precedence for publishing. John Wesley, the founder of Methodism, published 5,000 sermons, pamphlets and books. Probably his most famous works, aside from his sermons, were about abolishing slavery and providing health care. In Detroit, Father Gabriel Richard, a Catholic priest, and his Presbyterian friend Rev. John Monteith started a printing operation prior to co-founding what would become the University of Michigan.

Needless to say, the other reason for launching this new venture is that it will provide employment and an independent funding stream for our work.

Finally, writing this book has changed me. I consider myself a speaker rather than a writer. Much of my career has been spent fundraising, which has caused me to self-censor more often than not. I am also naturally an introverted and private person. The writing process was cathartic.

Map of Detroit

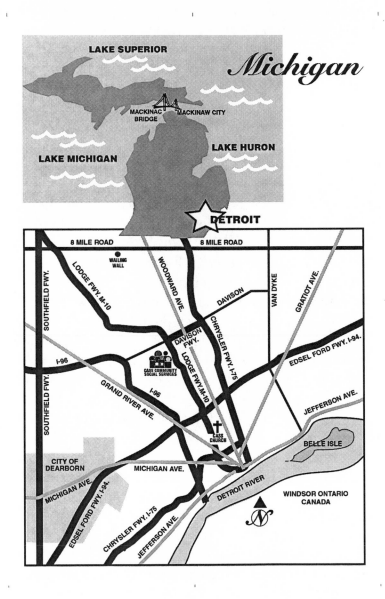

Acknowledgements

Although writing is a solitary process, a number of people motivated and advised me from the book's inception until the end.

I am indebted to Desiree Cooper who urged me to tell the Cass story, Julie Fitzsimmons who helped me avoid procrastination and Candy Zann who copy edited the text.

I can't say enough about the tremendous support from Cass staff members: Mary Burns, Kim Conwell, Ed Hingelberg, Pat DeCarlo, Terra Linzner, Pat McCaffrey-Green, Tashon McDuffie, Polly McCalister and Sue Pethoud.

Valuable content feedback came from a host of professional journalists, professors and friends including Mercedes Clingerman, Dr. Mary Collar, Rev. Laurie Haller, Judy Harnish, Dr. Robert Hoag, Bonnie Melendez and Louise Travis.

Read The Spirit founder, David Crumm, and his incredible colleagues, Dmitri Barvinok, John Hile, Patty Thompson and Joe Grimm deserve credit for editing, formatting, designing, proofreading and printing the book and making it available on demand and as an e-book.

Finally, I am grateful for the generous endorsements from giants Mitch Albom, Dr. Karen Oliveto, Neal Rubin and Pastor Rudy Rasmus, and the marketing genius of Marcy Hayes.

About the Author

Faith Fowler was born and raised in Detroit. Her teenage years were spent in Royal Oak, Michigan. She has degrees from Albion College, Boston University School of Theology and the University of Michigan-Dearborn. Her interests include reading, running, traveling and photography. This is her first book.

CPSIA information can be obtained
at www.ICGtesting.com
Printed in the USA
LVOW12s1302151216

517410LV00003B/94/P

9 781939 880703